Prai

"Melanie Ellison has done homeschool grads (and, truly, *all* high school students) a great favor by pulling together research, analysis of modern educational trends, and personal stories from the battlefront of 'higher' education. If you're standing at the fork in the road wondering which way to go, grab a copy of *Chucking College* today. Or if you're a parent who isn't sure what alternatives are out there to the (expensive) brick-and-mortar option, please read this book. Well done, Melanie!"

—JENNIE CHANCEY, founder of Ladies Against Feminism, coauthor of *Passionate Housewives Desperate for God*

"While I am a profound advocate of 'higher education' let it be known that I am a profound advocate of *higher* education. What is presently being offered by America's colleges and universities majoring in 'party' or 'marijuana day' is not even 'lower education.' And these 'educational' institutions fostering warmed-over atheism, relativism, and evolutionism are propaganda mills and not related to any definition of 'higher education.' Therefore, what Miss Ellison is seeking to do with *Chucking College* is well worth reading and her Appendix B entitled 'College Dropouts Hall of Fame' is worth the price of the book.

—DAVID A. NOEBEL, former president of Summit Ministries

Continued...

"There are 100 reasons to reconsider the college paradigm. Melanie Ellison is ahead of the curve with ... *Chucking College*. The paradigm is shifting fast. It is high time to examine how the average college situation today fails to provide mentorship, practical know-how, market preparedness, a proper biblical worldview, and spiritual and life maturity for young men and women."

—KEVIN SWANSON, *Generations Radio* host

"Is going to college the way to success? Or, is it becoming obsolete in the new wave of the future? Melanie Ellison meticulously researches this topic in her book— statistically, financially, politically, biblically, and with testimonies. I believe every parent and 'college contemplating student' must read this book with open eyes before making their final decision. Why stay in the rut when there are greater success options available?"

—NANCY CAMPBELL, founder of *Above Rubies*

Chucking

COLLEGE:

Achieving Success Without Corruption

MELANIE ELLISON

Devoted Maidenhood

All Scripture quotations are taken from the New King James Version, unless otherwise noted.

Cover design by Erin Jones, www.piebirdcreative.com.

Library of Congress Cataloging-in-Publication Data
Ellison, Melanie, 1990-
 Chucking college : How to achieve success without corruption / Melanie Ellison.
 Durango, Colo.: Devoted Maidenhood, c2012.
 268 p.; 22 cm.
 ISBN-10: 0-9882835-5-7
 ISBN-13: 978-0-9882835-5-8
 1. High school graduates -- United States -- Life skills guides
 2. Education -- Women 3. Universities and colleges -- Moral and ethical aspects -- United States. 4. Teenagers -- Vocational guidance.
 LB2350 .E45 2012
 378.73 ELL 2012

DEDICATION

To you dear young ladies who seek the heavenly Father's
will with all your heart and desire not to be corrupted
through higher education. My prayer is that He will give
you guidance in this next exciting stage of your lives.

TABLE OF CONTENTS

INTRODUCTION

The very first battle mankind had was over higher education in the garden of Eden. Adam and Eve put God's purpose for them—to take dominion and be fruitful and multiply—aside for the sake of man-centered higher education.[1] As Genesis 3:4-6 recounts:

> Then the serpent said to the woman, "You will not surely die. For God knows that in the day you eat of [the tree of knowledge] your eyes will be opened, and you will be like God, knowing good and evil." So when the woman saw that the tree was good for food, that it was pleasant to the eyes, and a tree desirable to make one wise, she took of its fruit and ate. (Genesis 3:4-6)

So the question continues. Will today's form of the tree of knowledge—the college experience—cause our faith to surely die? In answering that question, will we fall into believing Satan's lie that seeking humanistic higher education will *not* harm us? Or will we listen to the specific warnings of our Creator through His Word? Social pressure and appeal to ego caused Eve to fall, and those are still the two ploys the enemy uses today in his attempt to lure Eve's daughters into faith-eroding colleges.

Many Christian leaders and authors realize how detrimental the college setting has become, but their conclusion is, "...so *when* you go, pray extra hard, and be aware." However, we cannot afford to take that track any more. We have to grapple with the fact that 50-80% of students lose their faith at college. Enough casualties exist to prove that it is not worth remaining in the line of fire; statistically, the backsliding rate equals 4 out of 5 at worst and 1 out of 2 at best. Young people can hope to remain in the 20% whose faith still stands when they graduate, or they can drastically increase their chances of staying strong by not immersing themselves in the university cesspool.

College does have its advantages. But the accompanying devastating costs may no longer be worth sacrificing for the limited gain. As the Savior said, "For what will it profit a man if he gains the whole world, and loses his own soul?" (Mark 8:36). The point of this book is not to say that it is impossible to survive as a believer or to get a rigorous education at college, but rather to reveal that doing so is rare. Some may find that the path God has for them involves college, but the headlong assumption that *every* high school graduate who wants to avoid failure must automatically follow the traditional route deserves questioning.

I, personally, was warned about going to college prior to enrolling, but honestly, I had no desire to stay at home and waste my life away, so I went, not seeing any better option. After waking up to the reality that my college was not at all an arena in which a believer could thrive, I chucked college and came home. Not finding a book that explored avenues of success as alternatives to college, I began researching for myself. When my compiled research and personal experience reached seventy pages, I had to admit that a book was being born. The responsibility to share this information with others burned within me, and I had no choice but to continue writing.

This book is for young ladies and their parents. Because of the direction of 1 Timothy 2:12, it is not my place as a woman to teach men, so girls, this book is all yours. Because some of the content may be a bit shocking regarding the nature of sin on college campuses, you will probably want to have one of your parents read it before you if you are younger than eighteen. Regardless, hold open conversations with your parents about the topics in this book. Rather than being inappropriate, discussing such material as presented within the first half of this book is vital. If a young lady is not warned about college immorality (in the dorms *and* classrooms) and given the choice to knowledgably turn from such an environment ahead of time, she will experience the blatant flaunting of such wickedness daily after she is enrolled. So, unfortunately, in this godless day, the choice is not *whether* to hear this information, but *when*. It is so much better to be exposed to worldliness with your parents from outside of the eroding environment rather than alone from within it.

The facts presented in this book are generalizations based on the vast majority of universities, secular and

Christian, public and private. A very, very, small handful of colleges still stand strong, but these are so rare as to be almost nonexistent.

This book is not for those who have their hearts set on going to college. This book exists to validate those who are having misgivings about investing four to eight years on a diploma that may not even result in a job or a quality education.

The personal stories in the grey boxes throughout this book provide confirmation that others have felt similarly about college, and they offer encouraging evidence that a person can be successful without college—sometimes even more so than with it.

1

SPIRITUAL TSUNAMI

*"And Jesus answered and said unto them,
'Take heed that no man lead you astray.' "
(Matthew 24:4 ASV)*

Liberal thinkers have hijacked most colleges today and turned them into tsunamis that surge against the faith of students. Though Christian students swim tenaciously against the tide for a while, statistics show that most of them do not stand a chance against the tsunami, but emerge from college robbed of their foundational biblical beliefs.

For a year, I attended a supposedly Christian college—one that had daily chapel services and required Bible courses. I add the word "supposedly" because the true state of Christianity on campus proved less than desirable. Though the college held chapel services, they were not the place to go to strengthen one's faith. Still, I tried to go to chapel every once in a while, thinking that the previous time I had gone must have been a bad sampling.

In one such service, as the pipe organ swelled out the beginning chords of the hymn, "Give to our God Immortal Praise," my heart rose in worship, and I began to sing gustily. Gustily, that is, until I clamped my mouth shut at the verses that began to call on "mother earth, brother wind, brother fire, and most gentle sister death." My mind whirled as the congregation continued to sing; *surely those words were typos*, I hoped. But, upon looking around, I discovered that my fellow worshippers did not have similarly shocked countenances—indeed, they did not act like anything peculiar had transpired at all! When the lyrics finally moved on to the "alleluias," I unlocked my jaw and rejoined in singing (I was a little confused, however, as to why everyone sang alleluia—"praise God"—when everything *but* God had just been extolled). As soon as the service was over, I quickly made my exit, my conclusion reinforced that chapel service really was *not* the place to find biblically sound encouragement. Rather, chapel offered the time and place to call on one's own goodness, and to feel united with nature.

Often, the church building on campuses (if there is one) is the worst place to seek biblical encouragement. Angelic and demonic spirits rage over college chapels in an all-out battle for the souls beneath the roof. Chapel buildings commonly host interfaith dialogs (where atheistic and Islamic truth gain increasing prominence), often become the stage for homosexuals in leadership, and frequently are pulpits of evolution, New Age doctrine, and humanism.

Several universities and colleges (even Christian ones) have banned InterVarsity Christian Fellowship and Campus Crusade for Christ from having a presence on their campus. One such exclusion took place in December of 2011 at the University of New York in Buffalo. The university's reason was that InterVarsity "discriminates" by not allowing homosexuals to take leadership positions in their faith-based events (though as a Christian organization, they should have the right to determine who fills leadership positions).

On other campuses, no reason is given for not allowing Christian organizations on campus, other than that the campus has its own student faith center, and does not want an outside group that it cannot control. Sadly, college-based ministries are often student-run and do not have the maturity to adequately deal with the soul-wrenching dilemmas of student life at college. Consequentially, when Christian students feel their faith being eroded academically and socially, they often do not have a dependable place to go to spiritually recharge and find biblical answers for tough questions.

Legacy of the Ivy League

Colleges were not always this rough on students' faith. In fact, all of America's Ivy League colleges were founded for very godly reasons, which makes it all the more shocking to see how far they have fallen. Let us take a look at their exemplary Christian roots.

Harvard University was the first institution of higher learning in the U.S. colonies—a Puritan minister founded it in 1636. John Harvard's intention in establishing the university was to more adequately train Christian ministers. In accordance with that vision, Harvard's "Rules and Precepts" (adopted in 1646) stated:

> Let every Student be plainly instructed, and earnestly pressed to consider well, the maine end of his life and studies is, to know God and Jesus Christ which is eternal life (John 17:3) and therefore to lay Christ in the bottome, as the only foundation of all sound knowledge and learning.[1]

Since 1692, Harvard's motto has been, "Veritas Christo et Ecclesiae," meaning, "Truth for Christ and the Church."

Ten other ministers founded **Yale University** in 1701, and they established the school with a surprisingly similar focus. Their primary goal stated: "Every student shall consider the main end of his study to wit to know God in Jesus Christ and answerable to lead a Godly, sober life." In 1802, a faculty member named Benjamin Silliman commended the godliness of the school in a letter to his mother. He wrote, "prayer and praise seem to be the delight of the greater part of the students."[2]

Moving forward in history, in 1746, **Princeton University**, like Harvard, was established for the specific purpose of training ministers. The first president, Jonathan Dickinson, once stated in regard to the school, "Cursed be all learning that is contrary to the cross of Christ."

The seal of **Columbia University** (founded in 1754) displays several biblical components. The reference, "1

Peter 2:1-2" underlies the image of a woman on a throne with three little boys at her feet. The verse reads, "Therefore, laying aside all malice, all deceit, hypocrisy, envy, and all evil speaking, as newborn babes, desire the pure milk of the Word, that you may grow." This lady, who symbolizes wisdom, holds an open Bible in her right hand with the words "Logia Zonta" ("the living Word") prominently displayed on the pages. The Hebrew Name of God—Yahweh—stands boldly at the top of the emblem. The school's motto, "In Lumine Tuo Videbimus Lumen," which means, "In Your light we see light" (Psalms 36:9), arcs across the top. Finally, out of the lady Wisdom's mouth is a label with the words "Auri Al," ("God is my Light") alluding to Psalm 27:1 ("The Lord is my light and my salvation").

And lastly, **Dartmouth College** (founded in 1769) grew from the noble intent of educating and empowering missionaries to the Indians. Dartmouth's motto is: "Vox Clamantis in Deserto," which, translated from the Latin means, "The voice of one crying in the wilderness"— alluding to John the Baptist preparing the way of the Messiah. Dartmouth's insignia prominently contains the Hebrew words "El Shaddai" (God Almighty).

Downfall

Though their biblical heritage was upright, the departure of these institutes of higher learning from their pure foundations has been drastic. Following is a sampling of how far the Ivy League universities have fallen.

Today the Harvard Divinity School's master's program offers focuses in Buddhist Studies, Hinduism, Islam (including a course on Satanic verses that is not open to auditors—wonder why?), and specific courses such as "Feminist Biblical Interpretation," "Theology in an Interreligious Perspective," "Strategies for Worship in Postmodernity," "Bodies and Sexuality in the Medieval Middle East," and other such deviant titles. So much for striving to know God as the main end of their studies.

The 2011-2012 Yale course catalog boasted no less than twenty-eight courses in LGBT (Lesbian, Gay, Bisexual, and Transgender) studies. As a whole, Yale's students can no longer be described as delighting in prayer and praise.

Not all colleges have such outspoken course titles that blatantly reveal their stance on spiritual issues. Innocent enough titles such as "Introduction to the New Testament" often conceal faith-eroding teachings, as we will discuss in a later chapter.

Analyzing the downfall of America's best colleges helps to understand what has happened to the rest of them. The most prestigious colleges lead, and less well-known colleges follow suit.

College Testimony from History: David Brainerd (1718-1747), missionary to American Indians

(As this story reveals, even from the beginning of the Ivy League's history, colleges were never the best environments for spiritual vitality.)

"Guided with the purpose of furnishing himself completely unto the work of the ministry, Brainerd entered Yale College [in] September, 1739. He doubted his ability to lead a life of strict religion in the midst of temptations incident to student life. He knew Yale was then in a spendthrift era of morals, money, and wit; but this was not what he feared. The hours of study required were the dangerous factors: these might cause him to lose the sweet relish of faith and grow dull towards religion. ...

In January, 1740, an epidemic of measles swept the campus. ... After he contracted [it], he became so ill he was obliged to return to the ... farm. And there ... his affection for God flamed brighter than ever ... When he thought of going back to college and its attendant dangers of getting away from God, he would rather have died.

However, in late January, he returned to Yale. ... But the rowdy atmosphere among the students disturbed him more than he thought it would. It was like poison. One day in June 1740, [while walking in] the fields alone, he found unspeakable sweetness in God: the vulgar life of the students presumed to be Christians seemed unintelligible—and intolerable. He felt obliged to isolate himself from it. Therefore he decided to plunge into hard study, but this was a serious mistake. He greatly wronged his health and his spirituality."[3]

—RICHARD ELLSWORTH DAY, *Flagellant on Horseback*

Students Leaving the Faith

The anti-faith college tsunami is devastatingly effective. Most recent studies conclude that 50%-80% of students abandon their faith during college. Conservatives are emerging as liberals; once-vibrant Christians are doubting the inspiration of the Bible.

The Higher Education Research Institute states about college students: "36 percent rate their spirituality *lower* after three years in college… Comparing the responses of freshmen who checked the 'born again' category with the answers they gave four years later, 59 percent no longer describe themselves as 'born again.' "[4]

The Barna Research Group found in 2006 that "a majority of twentysomethings—61% of today's young adults—had been churched at one point during their teen years but they are now spiritually disengaged (i.e., not actively attending church, reading the Bible, or praying). Only one-fifth of twentysomethings (20%) have maintained a level of spiritual activity consistent with their high school experiences."[5]

In 2003, The Higher Education Research Institute at UCLA conducted a national study with 3,680 junior year students.[6] Their discoveries showed that "52% of college students reported frequent church attendance the year before they entered college but only 29% continued frequent church attendance by their junior year."[7]

"To uncover the reasons young people leave church, LifeWay Research conducted a survey in April and May 2007 of more than 1,000 adults ages 18-30. Each indicated that they had attended a Protestant church regularly for at least a year in high school. ... According to the study, 70 percent of young adults ages 23-30 stopped attending church regularly for at least a year between ages 18-22." They listed their reasons for doing so. Fifty-two percent stated that they stopped attending church because of "religious, ethical or political beliefs," implying that those beliefs changed at college.[8]

College Testimony from History: John Wesley (1703-1791), cofounder of the Methodist Church

"Oxford did little to improve John's spiritual life. In reality the university had struck one of the low levels of its scholastic and religious history and had little to offer a student save a boarding place." As he said of his time studying there, " 'I had not, all this while, so much as a notion of inward holiness; nay, went on habitually and for the most part very contentedly in some or other known sin.' "[9]

—BASIL MILLER, *John Wesley*

These statistics are alarming but certainly not exaggerated. One has only to think of the number of peers one personally knows who headed into college with a heart beating for their Creator only to graduate with a changed identity that matched the world more than the Savior. They confirm the statistics.

If young people keep going into the tsunami that is knocking down so many, what will be the state of the church in one generation? Ashamedly, "there's a higher percentage of practicing Christians in Communist China than at Penn State[.]"[10] One out of every two believers (if not more) emerge devastated after a ride through the spiritual pounding. Their faith has been wrenched from their hands through wave after wave of battering.

Even Christian Colleges

Shocking though it may be, even most *Christian* colleges rarely teach Christianly and are not innocent of attacking students' faith. As the book *Already Compromised* (based on Answers in Genesis' survey of 200 Christian colleges) revealed:

> What we appear to have is a basic biblical illiteracy among some of the leaders and professors of Christian colleges. Not only are their responses [in the survey] contradictory to the clear teachings of Scripture, but they are also inconsistent with themselves. [11]

Through careful questioning, the survey uncovered that while presidents and professors at Christian colleges may state that they believe the Bible is literally true, "when you ask them specific questions related to the truth of Scripture, [you] find out that many of them don't believe that at all."[12] Specifically, the discrepancy between what they say and what they believe manifested in areas such as creation (vs. evolution) and scriptural inerrancy.

Therefore, "parents are sending their students into [Christian colleges] assuming that they are going to be faith-nurturing and truth-affirming institutions. In reality, many of them discredit faith, discredit the Bible, and break kids down rather than build them up."[13] Author Ken Ham continues, "If you send your child to a Christian university, three out of four times they will stand in front of teachers who have a degraded view and interpretation of Scripture."[14]

College Testimony: Christian College Equally Bad

"I attended a supposed 'Christian' University for part of my college years. I was under the impression I would find godly friends there who were ready to grow up from all the public school baggage! Well, I was shocked to find out that the kids were the same, the sins were the same, and I struggled to be separate. The godlessness was abounding, the professors were liberal, and I often found myself just sitting in quiet disagreement. Anyone who spoke out for our faith would be immediately ridiculed. I was definitely influenced and it took me years to recover.

I still had a strong faith, but I was influenced to live and think more like the world—specifically, thinking I had to have a career. That thinking automatically makes women believe children are of secondary importance, which is a terrible lie that the system encourages.

At the end of five years of college the Lord opened my eyes to the evil and demonic influences in the field of Psychology that I was studying. So, there I was with a bachelor's degree in a field I wanted nothing to do with! I know all things work for the

---

good of those who love Him, but that doesn't mean there aren't consequences. Even my marriage has suffered as a result of college, because for many years I felt I deserved to be in charge, which caused resentment in my husband. I would not want my daughter to go to college, and especially don't want her to live on campus or with peers. I just don't think it's worth the moral consequences.

I believe parents are brainwashed into thinking that their kids have to have a college degree to succeed. It's just not true. My father, brothers, and my husband are all without degrees, yet they have successful businesses and their wives are able to stay home. The Lord provides!"

—TENISA MADDOX, wife and mother of three

So, sadly, even in many higher education arenas that claim to be bastions of Christian thought, the faith of students finds little refuge from attack. Some have pointed out that students' spiritual vitality may be safer at a secular university, because there at least they would have their guard up. At a Christian college, students *expect* biblical teaching; thus they are not prepared when the authority of the Bible is torn to shreds in the classroom under the guise of "academia." As Greg Hall (coauthor of *Already Compromised*) states, "the spiritual well-being for many students is hindered and not enhanced while attending Christian schools."[15] He knows what he is talking about, because he is the president of a Christian college himself.

It's Calculated

The destruction of students' faith is not an accident. College administrators are fully aware of the erosion that takes place. Indeed, they are sympathetic to the process, and they have designed it. A large part of the effectiveness of their method comes from the emphasis for students to cut ties with their anchor—Dad and Mom. Colleges know that if a student is not connected to a strong anchor to keep pulling them back to family values, they will go adrift when godless ideologies hit them. Then the university professors will be free to have the most impact in their anchorless lives.

Some have been vocal about this subterfuge. Woodrow Wilson (who was president of Princeton University before he was president of the United States), said in a speech in 1914, "I have often said that the use of a university is to make young gentlemen as unlike their fathers as possible."[16]

One of the presidents of Dartmouth College—James O. Freedman—agreed with Wilson's statement, and in his commencement address in 2002 he boldly stated, "the purpose of a college education is to question your father's values."[17] Therefore, from freshman orientation on, parents are expected to leave and be out of the way of the administrations' agenda.

In his book, *Inside American Education,* the insightful author Thomas Sowell wrote, "Advocates of secular humanism, for example, have been quite clear and explicit as to the crucial importance of promoting their philosophy in the schools, *to counter or undermine religious values* among the next generation."[18]

The late Richard Rorty, a postmodernist (one who believes that there are no objective standards) philosopher who was a professor at Yale, Princeton, and finally Stanford, had several very revealing comments about the goal of many college professors:

> I, like most Americans who teach humanities or social science in colleges and universities ... try to arrange things so that students who enter as bigoted, homophobic, religious fundamentalists will leave college with views more like our own.

> ... When we American college teachers encounter religious fundamentalists, we do not consider the possibility of reformulating our own practices of justification so as to give more weight to the authority of the Christian scriptures. Instead, we do our best to convince these students of the benefits of secularization. We assign first-person accounts of growing up homosexual to our homophobic students for the same reasons that German schoolteachers in the postwar period assigned *The Diary of Anne Frank.*

> ... There are credentials for admission to our democratic society, credentials which we liberals have been making more stringent by doing our best to excommunicate racists, male chauvinists, homophobes, and the like. You have to be educated in order to be a citizen of our society, a participant in our conversation, someone with whom we can envisage merging our horizons. *So we are going to go right on trying to discredit you in the eyes of your children, trying to strip your fundamentalist religious community of dignity, trying to*

make your views seem silly rather than discussable. We are not so inclusivist as to tolerate intolerance such as yours.

... I don't see anything herrschaftsfrei [domination-free] about my handling of my fundamentalist students. Rather, I think those students are lucky to find themselves under the benevolent Herrschaft [domination] of people like me, and to have escaped the grip of their frightening, vicious, dangerous parents.[19]

"For the leaders of this people cause them to err, and those who are led by them are destroyed."
(Isaiah 9:16 KJV)

In a lecture entitled "University of Babylon," Jeff Shafer, an attorney with the Alliance Defending Freedom, quoted the administration of the University of Ohio as stating, "It is precisely to skewer the conventional wisdom of students that we have this summer required reading." His response was that this is "unquantifiably preposterous." Shafer also stated, "Universities are operations that are militantly against Christians. They aim to strip your religion of dignity and make it despicable instead of discussable."[20]

I had an opportunity to personally experience the deadness of students' faith on the Collegiate Day of Prayer. I sent out an email appeal to my fellow students (only those who were Christians) to fast and pray for repentance in our hearts and on our campus, or at the very least to meet for a prayer meeting during the chapel break when no classes were held. None of these people attended chapel regularly, because of the spiritual deadness there, so I knew this would be a good time to meet for earnest prayer as a group. I was extremely dumbfounded when only two young ladies showed up. One left after five minutes—she said that she had some things she had to get done. The faith of the students on campus was dried up. It was nowhere near the top of their list of priorities.

Advance of Islam Through Colleges

One of the more powerful ideological tsunami waves that universities are allowing on their campuses is Islam. Dr. Anis Shorrosh identifies this agenda in the following Islamic goals recounted in his article, "Twenty-Year and Twenty-Step Plan for USA—Islam Targets America."

11. Provide very sizeable monetary Muslim grants to colleges and universities in America to establish 'Centers for Islamic studies' with Muslim directors to promote Islam in higher education institutions.
17. Raise interest in Islam on America's campuses by insisting that freshman take at least one course on Islam. Be sure that the writer is a bonafide American, Christian, scholarly [type] and able to cover up the violence in the Quran and express the peaceful, spiritual and religious aspect only.[21]

Thus, universities provide a major platform for Islam. There is even an organization called "Islam on Campus" that exists to prompt students to embrace Islam and reject Christianity.

Pluralism—A Stepping-Stone

The guise of religious pluralism is one technique those behind this agenda utilize to bring Islam onto an equal platform with other religions on campus. However, religious pluralism is a position that cannot logically be maintained. To assert that all religions are equal is to say that they present equally valid truth claims about the world. The problem is, religious truth claims contradict each other. Christianity holds the position that Jesus is the Son of God and equal to God, while Mormons believe He is the brother of Lucifer, and Muslims relegate Him to the level of a prophet. These positions cannot all be true simultaneously.

Or take the differing views on how to make it to heaven. These three religions each exclusively state that entrance into heaven is accomplished a different way. The Bible says by "grace alone, not through works" (Eph. 2:9-10), while the LDS Third Article of Faith claims that good works form the integral part: "all mankind may be saved, by obedience to the laws and ordinances of the gospel" (*Pearl of Great Price*), and the Hadith, the second most important Islamic holy book (after the Quran) states, "The person who participates in Jihad ... will be admitted to paradise" (Hadith, Vol 1:35). So, we see, if one is true, by implication the other two are false. If a person can *only* make it to heaven by acts of jihad, then they cannot *only* get there by the Messiah's saving grace. When two ideas are mutually exclusive, they cannot both be true.

Thus, it is impossible for all religions to be equally valid. *If all religions are right, then they are all wrong.* Yet, students accept pluralism because it is emotionally satisfying to be inclusive of all views rather than to point out the logical fact that one position must be wrong.

Islam—Egalitarian?

Once Islam is accepted through the stepping-stone of pluralism, people cease to see anything dangerous about Islam. Colleges are careful to present it as an egalitarian religion. Yes, egalitarian—the belief that all people deserve equal rights. Not quite the word that automatically comes to mind when thinking of Islam.

Before I even reached my college campus, I was required to read an autobiography of a Muslim for a summer reading assignment. The book was titled: *Acts of Faith: The Story of an American Muslim, in the Struggle for the Soul of a Generation.* The subtitle with these revealing words: "the struggle for the soul of a generation" was left off of our reading guide. In fact, I hardly noticed it until I left college and regained my objectivity about what was really going on there. This book was an ideal first step (from the college administration's perspective) in helping Islam achieve its status as a religion as good as any other in the minds of incoming freshman.

As I read the book, I began to get a little confused. I had always thought that Islam was rather oppressive toward those who did not believe in their worldview, and especially so toward their women. But according to the book, I must have been mistaken. Astonishingly, on page 111, the author wrote: "the core message of Islam is the establishment of an ethical, egalitarian order on earth," and on page 113 it discusses "his interpretation of Islam as a nonviolent tradition of *liberation*" (emphasis added).

So, to make sure that I had not imagined all the persecution that I had thought came as a result of Muslims being loyal to the teaching of the Qur'an, I read some passages taken directly out of the Qur'an itself. The quotes I found did *not* strike an egalitarian tone. For example, I read Qur'an 4:34: "As to those women on whose part ye fear disloyalty and ill-conduct, admonish them (first), (Next), refuse to share their beds, (And last) beat them (lightly)." Another passage declares: "Fight and slay the Pagans [those who do not follow Allah] wherever you find them, and seize them, beleaguer them, and lie in wait for them in every stratagem (of war)" (Qur'an 9:5). How could this be called an egalitarian religion? Yet, as I finished the book, it was evident that the author presented Islam in exactly that way in order to cause students to ignorantly accept Islam in a first step toward discarding Christianity.

When I arrived at college, who did I discover to be the opening convocation speaker, but Eboo Patel, the author of the book. I went to the convocation begrudgingly, but took notes furiously through his whole message, expressing my responses within the safe confines of my notepad. I was surrounded by a thousand or two students who were hanging on, taking in, and extolling every remark of his.

A day or so later, in my very first class period, we were told right then and there to write what we thought of the book. Sweating bullets (I did not know but that we would have to turn in our papers immediately after class without being able to really weigh our words), I knew I was caught. I could laud the pluralistic position to gain a good grade, or I could write what I truly thought. I debated with my blank paper for a few minutes while those around me plunged ahead with strokes of the pen. Precious time fled from me. I anticipated the worst consequences that could come from writing against Islam. I knew it was fully possible that I could be expelled for taking a position opposite to that of the book (looking back, perhaps expulsion would not have been so bad as I thought). But my conscience was screaming, so with my heart in my throat, I began laying out case after case from the book and the Qur'an to prove that Islam is not in essence egalitarian.

I did not end up being thrown out of college for my views. However, when I received my paper back from the professor later, it was covered in rebuttals defending Islam. I was even more shocked at this response when I learned that my professor was a pastor of a local evangelical church! Through this incident, I learned firsthand the force that exists behind Islam on campus.

Once people accept Islam through the non-confrontational platform offered by religious pluralism, it becomes evident that the pluralistic front was simply a step in the process of moving people to reject all other religions in favor of Islam. Omar Ahmed, Chairman of the Board of the Council on American-Islamic Relations, makes this blatantly clear. He said, "Islam isn't in America to be equal to any other faith, but to become dominant. The Koran should be the highest authority in America, and Islam the only accepted religion on Earth."[22]

Asserting that Islam is the *only* way leads to tolerating "death to the infidel!" as the Qur'an requires—referring to anyone and everyone who does not follow Mohammad. The general view is that only radical Muslims support terrorist acts. However, the vast majority of Muslims, even of so-called peaceful Islamic sects, will tell you that if it came up for election, they absolutely would vote for Sharia law to be instituted. Sharia law involves active discrimination against and punishment of Jews and Christians, along with anyone else who will not acquiesce to the Islamic worldview. Sharia law manifests itself in very violent forms, such as beating, execution, and cutting off the hands of thieves. So, there is no such thing, ultimately, as a peaceful sect of Islam (as colleges would like students to believe). As Geert Wilders, leader of the Dutch Freedom Party stated:

> Muslims want you to make way for Islam, but Islam does not make way for you. The Government insists that you respect Islam, but Islam has no respect for you. Islam wants to rule, submit, and seeks to destroy our Western civilization. [23]

By mass indoctrination through colleges, Islam is succeeding in that very goal. According to one survey, "Only 16 percent [of college students] believe Western culture is superior to Arab culture, and 79 percent do not."[24]

Many are not aware of how calculated the advance is. Thus, this dangerous ideology is allowed to encroach with free reign, and as a result more and more college students transfer their allegiances over to Islam. Israeli author David Rubin wrote about this in his book, *The Islamic Tsunami*:

Universities seem defenseless [against Islam]. Europe's vaunted higher education has been infiltrated and confronted with a force of rampant Islamic population growth and intensely passionate hatred. All the PhD's in France, England, Spain, and Holland can't help to find the solution for this ... short of confronting the dual plagues of Islamic intimidation and political correctness.[25]

This infiltration of universities is happening across the globe, not just in America.

Muslims think long-term. They have no problem with not realizing the fulfillment of their goals for several generations. But the time for the calculated spread of Islam to be halted is in the beginning stages. The first step is becoming aware of Islam's now vigorous presence on campuses around the world. It is one of the ways universities are corroding students' faith.

Swimming in the Tsunami

How is the college tsunami so effective in tearing down faith that only a slim few hold on? College sabotages students' relationships, bodies, spirits, and minds, thus battering the very areas in which believers are commanded to love and obey the Creator: "You shall love the Lord your God with all your heart, with all your soul, and with all your strength" (Deuteronomy 6:5).

The question for us now is not so much "How did universities fall away from godliness?" but rather "What is the place for us as young women since this is now the norm at most colleges?" Should we consent and pay good money to be barraged by one of these mighty tsunamis for four to eight years? There is no hope for those who swim in a tsunami—no matter how well they can usually swim.

The best way to "Take heed that no man lead you astray" (the epigram at the head of this chapter) is to leave the place where it is the administration's goal to do exactly that—lead young people astray from their biblical beliefs.

College Testimony: Faith Nearly Robbed

"I came so close to losing my faith at the University of Wisconsin that I could take you to the very spot where I almost said: 'Nuts to God!' And that was after previously attending a Bible College. I'm grateful to God for an eighty-six-year-old man who got a hold of me piece by piece. If it weren't for him, I don't know where my faith would be. I eventually founded Summit Ministries because I knew there were other young people out there who were also having their faith torn down at colleges."

—DAVID NOEBEL, president emeritus
of Summit Ministries, author of
Understanding the Times (Summit Press: 1991)

2

MORAL MAELSTROM

"... When vileness is exalted among the sons of men."
(Psalm 12:8)

In blogging the following words, one Christian young person aptly expressed what many feel, but may not have the courage to admit about how college affects them:

Over the course of attending only a semester of secular university, a river ... full of potential carved out a canyon of discovery [which was] then quickly sucked dry as I plummeted into a world I had no desire to be in nor was really ready for. I couldn't say it took me by surprise as I failed to keep my life stream nourished and protected. Still, I reached a place [where] I knew I did not want to dwell. Surrounded by darkness, my vision of helping redeem the world and myself became shrouded. Away from family and genuine and intentional relationships, it was one of those places in life where I really didn't know where I was going (or rather forgot) but I knew where I was at the time was not right. I fell into a chasm and I wanted out desperately.[1]

Tsunamis can generate maelstroms; in fact, the Japanese tsunami of 2011 did spawn a massive whirlpool in the sea. Relating this to college in a metaphoric sense, the spiritual tsunamis on campus often do generate moral maelstroms. As students have their confidence in biblical values removed, answers to *why* an action is moral or immoral are difficult to find. Thus consciences spin out like a confused whirlpool, dragging students down to drown in moral compromise.

Everything's Relative

The waters in a maelstrom swirl confusedly; they do not progress in a calculated direction. Everything is relative in such a whirlpool—first the water flows one direction and then the other, and no direction seems better than the others. This is what the vortex of an immoral free-for-all feels like on a college campus. The very language used in reference to morals reveals the maelstrom in each heart. Phrases like the following are daily fare on a college campus: "What's right to you is right to you, and what's right to me is right to me; just don't oppress me with your morality," or "Who's to say?" or, "There is no such thing as right or wrong, it's just a personal preference."

Seventy-three percent of college seniors polled in an April 2002 Zogby survey stated that their professors taught them that "what is right and wrong depends on differences in individual values and cultural diversity."[2] In other words, *objective* right and wrong do not exist.

This lack of recognizing any objective standard for morality becomes painfully evident when asking college students, "Was Hitler wrong to do what he did?" The shocking response of the majority is "I personally think Hitler was wrong, but I can't objectively say that he was wrong. That's just how I feel, and no, I wouldn't condemn him, I just wouldn't choose to live like he did. I don't know everything, so who am I to declare what is right and what is wrong?"

In one of the required classes that I had to take in college, we did a Holocaust study on the book *Eichmann in Jerusalem: A Report on the Banality of Evil*, by Hannnah Arendt. The entire thrust of the book presented the conviction that Adolf Eichmann, the key SS organizer of logistics for exterminating the Jews, was basically thoughtless and innocent of any crime. The fact that the word banal is in the subtitle signifies that Eichmann's facilitating the death of five million Jews in the Holocaust was essentially a trite happenstance, and not a somber, calculated misdeed.

I argued in my reading response paper that Eichmann actually *was* responsible for his actions, contrary to the position presented in the book. When I received my paper back after grading, the professor's comments evidenced yet again the relative position college professors have taken toward morality. She wrote the following at the end of my paper:

> Eichmann's acts were legal in Germany. We can still condemn them as immoral ... but if his conscience was so readjusted (and reinforced by society) that he in fact saw

his acts as right, is he morally guilty for not seeing them to be wrong when no one else did and they were legal?

By stating that, my professor made it seem as if *consensus* is the true determinant of right and wrong, and not an objective moral standard. She was not willing to state that killing *any* number of people makes one morally guilty, and being responsible for the death of five million people especially so. By the way, this professor was no post-modern extremist like Richard Rorty. To the contrary, she was supportive of Christianity, and had previously had us study the history of the King James Bible. Nevertheless, I think only if Eichmann had sent my professor's own mother to a death camp would she have been willing to condemn his actions as utterly wrong.

The lack of moral decisiveness caused by this relativistic view of morals is shocking in the academic arena of college. College professors have "elevated sensitivity over the love of truth" as Bradford Wilson said.[3]

Immoral Currents

As a natural progression, these relativistic academics spin into relativistic behavior, including impure boyfriend-girlfriend relationships, avoidance of marriage altogether, homosexual behavior, drinking parties, and immersion in drugs. David Kupelian, author of the revealing book, *The Marketing of Evil*, described college life as having "an almost surreal level of in-your-face sexual anarchy and promiscuity."[4] Let's take a look at how prevalent each of these Sodom-like behaviors currently are in university student life.

Homosexuality

Homosexuality is quickly becoming rampant on many campuses. Even at Christian colleges, the vast majority of students do not see anything wrong with showing lots of physical affection to students of their own sex. Many young ladies call it an expression of Christian sisterly love. Regardless of what label it is given, the *behavior* they are participating in is the same as homosexual behavior: long naps together in the same bed, unabashed cuddling on the couch, lots of hugs and hand holding, etc. When asked to describe how homosexuality would differ from the actions in which they are engaged, these young ladies are either ignorant of the indicative signs of homosexuality, or they describe homosexuality as involving the same behaviors with a fundamental difference—that they are acting out of Christian love (as if the motive justifies the behavior).

When girls leave home, many feel lonely at college. There, they receive no wise restraining input from adults, and any brake that has held their physical behavior back is instantly removed by the "liberty" of dorm life. This is a dangerous, slippery slope that many young ladies don't even know they are on. They would be shocked to understand that they are participating in homosexual actions that lead to homosexuality itself.

The enemy probably likes it this way. He likes that whether or not they call it homosexuality, increasing numbers of students are dabbling in same-sex behaviors. Then when he gets a chance on a campus "Coming-Out Day," he leverages all that accumulated time young people spent experimenting to try to convince them to identify with homosexuals.

In his epic book, *Freefall of the American University*, Jim Nelson Black writes, "We used to have standards of decency. Now the thought police have to protect the standards of indecency ... Homosexuality is sacred on campus."[5] It is so sacred that many universities do not simply provide counseling and direction for people who struggle with same-sex attraction, but they push the entire college community to completely embrace it.

In an article published in *Gay Today* called "The Crimson Letter: Harvard, Homosexuality and the Shaping of American Culture," Jesse Monteagudo wrote, "Harvard's own gay experience ... struggled into the light in the 1950s, '60s, and '70s, observable chiefly in the increasingly rebellious profile of gay students, faculty, and alumni ... they created a thriving gay subculture that in time would surface boldly." Back in 1891, the dean of the Harvard Arts and Sciences Graduate School stated " 'homosexual desire should be thought of as 'being itself a natural, pure and sound passion, as worthy of the reverence of all fine natures as the honorable devotion of husband and wife, or the ardor of bride and groom.' "[6]

The article, "Colleges as 'Boot Camps' For Gay Activists," quotes the president of SaveCalifornia.com as saying:

> "Queer Studies teaches you can do anything sexual you want without negative consequences or moral account-ability to God, and that you have no ability to choose whether or not to engage in sexual behaviors. This

philosophy essentially turns man into an animal, but less than an animal, because beasts follow God's natural order of sexuality."[7]

College studies teach that homosexual behavior is genetic. But science does not confirm that position. The article continues: " 'Homosexual researchers have even looked for a genome, such as can be found for Alzheimer's, but it's not there.' "[8] Contrary to the claim that homosexual behavior is natural and genetic, Scripture describes homosexuality as *unnatural* in Romans 1:26-27. Here Paul wrote:

> God gave them over to shameful lusts. Even their women exchanged natural sexual relations for unnatural ones. In the same way the men also abandoned natural relations with women and were inflamed with lust for one another. Men committed shameful acts with other men, and received in themselves the due penalty for their error.

So who has the final say? The Bible or college administrators? Campus groups exert strong peer pressure over students.

Christian Colleges and Homosexuality

At Wheaton College: In April 2011, an organization was started by gay and gay-supporting alumni from Wheaton College, one of the most historically conservative colleges in America. This is the college that educated Billy Graham, John Piper, Jim and Elizabeth Elliot, Todd Beamer, Josh McDowell, Phillip Yancey, and other influential Christian individuals. The LGBT organization is called OneWheaton, and their main letter, written to encourage current Wheaton students to let their homosexuality emerge, states, in part, "your [homo]sexual identity is not a tragic sign of the sinful nature of the world. ... After Wheaton our lives became stories of liberation."[9] Online, this letter has over seven hundred alumni signatures as of March 2012, which means that seven hundred individuals had been dealing with homosexual urges while at Wheaton.

It would not be doing the college justice to neglect to mention the firm yet gracious stand President Ryken took when OneWheaton visited campus to distribute copies of their letter. Dr. Ryken responded by sending out an email to the student body with verses stating what the Bible says about homosexuality, and he also stated "that the school would continue to respond to all sinful behaviors with the 'truth and grace' of Scripture."[10]

As an interesting side note, these OneWheaton alumni have not denied the faith; to the contrary, they call themselves evangelical gays, according to *Time Magazine*.[11] An organization called SoulForce also attempts to couple homosexual behavior with the Christian faith. SoulForce travels around to campuses and holds programs for this purpose, twisting the clear words of Scripture to justify sin.

According to an article entitled "Christian Colleges are Latest Target of Homosexual Activists," "reparative counseling is a common option before dismissal" of Wheaton students exhibiting homosexual behavior, so they are given a chance to change before being asked to leave.

This article also states, "A handful of current faculty members and administrators have privately expressed a more affirming view of homosexuality, but declined to be named." This is even more shocking. The fact that faculty at such a renowned evangelical college should side for behavior that the Bible calls sin is a tragedy indeed.

At Belmont University: In February 2011, the spotlight on the homosexual stage turned to Belmont University—a growing college in Nashville, Tennessee, which claims on their website to be "the largest ecumenical Christian university in America." Although the university's vision is "to be a leader among teaching universities, bringing together the best of liberal arts and professional education in a Christian community," the Belmont administration announced in early 2011 "that the school officially had recognized its first gay student organization."[12] The push for recognition of a homosexual group at Belmont had been insistent for months before the decision. In fact, the board had turned down the group twice, before finally giving in.

At Westmont College: In the same month, another Christian college—Westmont College in California— entered the struggle. The college's official mission states, "Westmont College is an undergraduate, residential, Christian, liberal arts community serving God's kingdom by cultivating thoughtful scholars, grateful servants and faithful leaders for global engagement with the academy, church and world," and the college's motto is: "Christ Holding Preeminence." This is obviously not a secular school.

However, in February 2011, "the student newspaper ... printed an open letter signed by 131 gay and gay-supportive alumni." They wrote in their letter, "We offer our names as proof that LGBT people do exist within the Westmont community."[13] This is incredible, because each incoming student is required to sign Westmont's Community Life Statement, agreeing not to participate in behaviors such as "occult practices, drunkenness, theft, profanity, and dishonesty. Such activities also include sexual relations outside of marriage *and homosexual practice.*"[14] This incident shows that even when the campus administration has a conservative policy regarding immorality, what actually goes on in the student body may be another matter.

At Harding University: Harding University, a Church of Christ school in Arkansas, states about their faith-based identity on their website:

> We are, at our core, a Christian university. The character, example, and concerns of Jesus Christ are the standards that shape us and chart the course for our future. ... Every professor who stands in front of a class, every coach who stands in front of a team, and every director who stands in front of a cast or a music group is to speak and lead as a man or woman of God.

However, even here, in a manner similar to OneWheaton, on March 2, 2011, Harding alumni published a website displaying a letter that began thus:

> I'm writing you on behalf of a group of former and current Harding University students who identify as gay or lesbian. We have collectively written and compiled a

zine about our experiences being gay and lesbian at Harding."[15]

In other words, they did not adopt a homosexual identity *after* graduation, but *while* attending the Christian university.

At Baylor University: Even at the "country's largest Baptist college," a university with around 15,000 students, an unofficial gay group is pushing for recognition, according to the *New York Times*. In the article "Even on Religious Campuses, Students Fight for Gay Identity," reporter Erik Eckholm writes:

> Adam R. Short, a freshman engineering student at Baylor University who is openly gay ... has fought, without success, for campus recognition of a club to discuss sexuality and fight homophobia. ... Despite the rebuff, more than 50 students continue to hold weekly gatherings of their Sexual Identity Forum ... "The student body at large is ready for this," said Saralyn Salisbury, *Ms.* Jones's *girlfriend* and also a senior at Baylor.[16]

Here again, the administration may be taking a stand, but since the student body is not, homosexuality gains ground.

Torturous for the Righteous

For the students who want to remain pure, being surrounded by sodomy makes that quite a challenge. Just as Lot "living among them day after day, was tormented in his righteous soul by the lawless deeds he saw and heard" (2 Peter 2:8 NIV), being surrounded by such wickedness becomes torturous to the righteous student. A young person's spirit begins to feel eroded as those who call evil good attack holiness day-in and day-out. In the book *Slouching Towards Gomorrah*, Robert Bork described this erosion:

> So unrelenting is the assault on our sensibilities that many of us grow numb, finding resignation to be the rational, adaptive response to an environment that is increasingly polluted and apparently beyond our control."[17]

As Matthew Henry, an eminent Bible commentator of the seventeenth and eighteenth centuries, wrote about immorality within a "Christian" environment, "What did it avail them that they had the ark of God in Shiloh when they had Sodom in their streets?"[18]

Anti-Marriage Climate

One day at college, I wandered from one dorm room to the next, looking for a screwdriver to borrow in order to fix my door hinge. Tucking my head into an open doorway, I presented my request, and waited for the occupant to find the screwdriver. While I stood just inside the door, I noticed a strange set-up over the bottom bunk bed in the room. A sheet was draped down from the upper bunk, hiding the lower bed from view. Inside that hideout, I distinctly heard both a male and a female voice. I was shocked.

Here were a guy and a girl in bed together with the door wide open, and the roommate acting like nothing unusual was occurring. Should I rip the sheet down, and expose the act like Phinehas did in the Bible when he plunged a sword through two blatant fornicators (Numbers 25:7-8)? Or should I just continue to pretend like this was normal, everyday life? Torn, I ended up leaving without saying anything, but grieving in my soul. There I was at a private Christian college, and no one's conscience motivated them to stand up and rebuke such behavior. I realized this was not an environment of academic advancement; this was Sodom.

On my own floor (a quiet, conservative one, compared to the other floors), three guys "lived" with their girl-friends. Of course, they did not room there officially, as the rules required guys and girls to leave each others' floors at 2 a.m., but no Resident Assistant (RA) enforced that. She would have been laughed at. So, there were those three guys—easy to identify as they left the girls' rooms groggy-eyed first thing in the morning, to head for the bathroom on the guys' floor just below.

College dorms are really not much different from red-light districts, if we honestly admit it. In life outside college, most godly girls are not surrounded by such a high concentration of immoral living. But in a dormitory, even if a student personally desires to remain pure, she has to endure how her roommates choose to live. Consequently, she finds herself exposed to indecency to which she never agreed and should never have had to endure. (Isn't it inter-esting that students are often required to live in campus dorms in the process of gaining *academic* credentials?)

Actions give ground to the spiritual forces of either God or the devil. Thus, the past ungodly actions within college dorms have given Satan legal ground to let loose his influence over current and future students. Hundreds of years of immorality have allowed well-entrenched demonic cauldrons to take root within dorm rooms, and that influence spawns more such behavior.

On most campuses, there is not even an expectation for students to remain physically pure. To the contrary, "exploration" is encouraged even before classes begin. During freshman orientation, supplies are handed out, and classes are taught, involving in-depth instruction on how to be immoral.

One young lady had to endure such an orientation after she was selected to be an RA at a "Christian" college. The icebreaker activity involved pairing up (guys and gals) and rubbing the body parts that the organizer called out. It began with rubbing elbows, and ended with rubbing behinds. She shared that the pressure to conform was so intense that for her to have stood apart from the activity after entering that orientation room would have taken superhuman resolve.

Harvard, Yale, and Dartmouth each host an annual Sex Week, with schedules full of seminars and events on topics too blatantly immoral to repeat. Some days contain seven or eight hours of workshops on wickedness. Does this not sound like Sodom? "They parade their sin like Sodom; they do not hide it" states Isaiah 3:9 (NIV). On campus, "premarital and homosexual sex are not debatable and may not be criticized,"[19] Jim Nelson Black pointed out.

The very root of all this immorality comes from the anti-marriage climate of college culture. A void always fills with something, and when 40% of Americans believe marriage is obsolete (according to a 2009 Pew study[20]), and consequently ridicule traditional husband and wife roles, it should not be surprising that rampant immorality fills the void. Currently, over 50% of children born to women under the age of thirty are born out of wedlock.[21] Marriage is no longer extolled as a good thing to pursue, so the God-given hormonal drive to find a mate becomes disconnected from its purpose and instead compels students to wallow in immorality.

A Mother's Perspective: RA's Police Evil

" Two of my daughters were RAs in college, and as a result of watching what they went through, I have come to see the position as one of policing evil—far from the privilege it was supposed to be. Universities give a financial reimbursement to students who will sign on to do their dirty work for them. They present the position as an honor, but it didn't turn out to be even 1% of what we envisioned. We thought being RAs would be a good ministry opportunity for our daughters, but we discovered that the resident girls didn't want mentoring. They wanted to be able to live immorally without consequences, and they had little respect for an RA who impeded their way. If our daughters caught the girls on their floor sneaking in their boyfriends at night or drinking, then our daughters were under pressure not to say anything, because these rule-breaking girls were their peers. RAs

---

are forced to see more immorality than others and are powerless to do much about it. It's an untenable position.

My daughters attended a Christian college, but even there, we felt like they were defiled of their innocence. It was the same feeling as the time when someone broke into our house and robbed us. We didn't raise our girls in purity their whole lives to have their innocence robbed at a Christian university. You can get education anywhere. When you send your children to a Christian college, there's a reason you send them to a Christian college. You're hoping for a Christian environment, but in the majority of cases it is not there.

Christian colleges can tend to present images of purity, but they fail to deliver up on their promises. I would love to play back what the president and dean promised us parents at orientation, because it turned out to be just a line; they didn't deliver. The college our daughters went to had every evil thing you would envision in a public university. It was not what we signed up for as parents."

—A MOTHER OF ELEVEN

Jennifer Roback Morse, founder of the Ruth Institute, which is dedicated to defending and promoting marriage on college campuses, said of the view of marriage on campus:

What [students] are getting on their campuses typically is an intellectual environment that is openly hostile to ...

traditional marriage. ... They're also facing ... a social climate which is actively promoting the hookup culture.[22]

When we look at Rome and other cultures that have preceded us down the path of tearing up the biblical family structure, we discover that no society survives the breakup of the family. The logical end of a civilization that embraces homosexuality, for instance, is extinction, because homosexuality does not result in procreation.

Why Young Women are Vulnerable

Young women find themselves vulnerable to relationships without commitment as a result of being out from under their fathers' authority, and as a result of finding themselves under a roof with free access to young men at all hours. Dorm life tempts young ladies as they fall into giving their hearts (and emotional and physical purity) to guys outside of marriage. Imagine the danger of living out years of raging hormones in a setting that imposes no moral limits or accountability on those hormones. This recipe for moral failure is the essence of college dorm life.

The desire to belong to someone is so strong for a young woman that it is easy for that yearning to overpower her logic. A woman was designed for a man to hold her heart at every part of life—when single, her heart is her father's, and when married, her husband's. Thus the danger of being out of daily fellowship with her dad causes a girl to want to transfer her heart to a young man her age, just as wifehood naturally follows daughterhood. The problem is, without her father's participation in picking the guy to which to give her heart in marriage, in desperation she gives it to anyone who will make her feel cherished, even temporarily. Before she knows it, she has gotten in too deep with the wrong guy.

Unhelpful College Habit #1: Self-Centeredness

College life develops the habit of living a self-centered life, one that avoids serving others when it is inconvenient (which it always is). Family life, on the other hand, forces one to get outside of oneself, and have empathy for those around them. Because of the bond of commitment within a family, one cannot just brush off others' needs as easily as in a college setting.

The college atmosphere not only discourages the idea of serving others (aside from an occasional mission trip—though anyone would agree that it takes much more self-discipline to serve one's own family than to serve the poor in the spotlight for a week), but it encourages a "you-serve-me" attitude. For example, a college student does not have to exert effort to fix her own dinner; she expects someone else to do that for her behind the scenes in the cafeteria. This type of college-generated narcissism only leads to disillusionment when students graduate and find that the world does not rotate around them after all.

In Randy Alcorn's excellent little book, *The Purity Principle*, he writes, "Run from temptation as from a slithering cobra or a live grenade."[23] Avoiding temptation is pursuing our own best self-interest; indulgence is not. It is very difficult to avoid temptation when immersed in it while separated from one's family at college. The solution is to leave the environment.

Perhaps it will feel like sacrifice to not be involved in the relational life that college offers. However, as Josh Harris encourages:

> God never calls us to sacrifice as an end in itself, but only through sacrifice on the way to great joy. On the other side of the seeming loss and denial is always reward and pleasure so deep and so intense that it's almost impossible to call what you gave up a sacrifice at all. And that's true even if the suffering and self-denial God calls us through lasts a lifetime.[24]

Drinking, Drugs, Music

These days, most college youth echo the shortsighted cry recorded in Isaiah 22:13: "Let us eat and drink, for tomorrow we die!" Few college students have an eternal mindset. They do not weigh the everlasting consequences that result from momentary pleasures, thus they take part in drinking, drugs, and rock music.

Drinking: In my freshman dorm at college, much drinking took place. It was illegal of course, because everyone was under age, but students drank anyway. In fact, before even reaching college, every incoming student was required to take a four-hour online course about how to drink "more responsibly." I do not remember anything in the course mentioning the fact that it is illegal to drink under the age of twenty-one.

Drugs: Some college students become hooked on so-called "smart" drugs such as Adderall and Ritalin to help them focus intently for hour after hour when studying. Though illegal to obtain without a prescription, through undercover markets and feigned ADHD one in five college students found a way to get Adderall.[25] This highly addictive drug can lead to such terrible side effects as hallucinations, suicide, irreversible schizophrenia, and bipolar disorder, but students are so driven to achieve good grades that they take the chance at the cost of their health.

Unhelpful College Habit # 2: Sleep Deprivation

Sufficient sleep is a joke among college students. Peers encourage each other, "If a project has to get done, stay up all night to do it! We all have to." Lack of sleep coupled with exposure to new germs and viruses weakens the immune system. No wonder 1 in 200 students contract mononucleosis. Insufficient sleep can also lead to "diabetes, cardiovascular diseases, obesity, and depression."[26] Sleep deprivation is not something to simply laugh away, but the pressure of homework deadlines and the tyranny of grades make it hard to avoid.

Music: Something else that bombards college students' spirits is the music blaring out of college dorm rooms. The type of music most young people in dorms listen to is not conducive to intellectual advancement or spiritual purity. As "Little Richard," one of the early musicians in the field of rock music, wrote:

> Rock 'n' roll doesn't glorify God. You can't drink out of God's cup and the devil's cup at the same time. I was one of the pioneers of that music, one of the builders. I know what the blocks are made of because I built them... I figure that rock 'n' roll is devastating to the mind. It is not from God. The lyrics don't talk about Jesus. The beat hypnotizes you.[27]

Even if Christian rock is the subject in question, the words and the music present a conflicting message. Rock music (with or without Christian lyrics) appeals to the *body*—just watch the sensual ways people are prompted to move while listening to it—whereas Christian lyrics appeal to the *soul*. Thus, the message is divided and the person has to choose whether to give in to sensuality or hold to spirituality.

On this topic, Andrew Pudewa's intriguing message, "The Profound Influence of Music on Life,"[*] is well worth hearing. In this presentation, he delivers the scientific findings of several studies involving rats listening to different kinds of music. The results of the experiments revealed that the rats that listened exclusively to rock music could not make it through the maze in which they were placed. They stumbled and operated in total confusion. (And, of course, lyrics make no difference to a

---

* Available from: www.excellenceinwriting.com/mus.

rat—they cannot discern the difference between Christian rock and secular rock.) On the other hand, the rats that heard strictly Mozart zipped through the maze even faster than the silence control group that heard no music at all. Therefore, the music most popular at institutions of higher learning not only wears on the soul of a believer, but it also limits the intellectual capabilities of students.

When John Wesley left home to go to college, he wrote his remarkably godly mother, Susanna Wesley, and asked her to define sin. This was her profound answer:

> Whatever weakens your reason, impairs the tenderness of your conscience, obscures your sense of God, takes away your relish for spiritual things, whatever increases the authority of the body over the mind, that thing is sin to you, however innocent it may seem in itself.

And so the question is: When we observe that the prevailing tendency of college life is indeed to weaken reason, impair conscience's tenderness, obscure the sense of God, take away relish for spiritual things, and increase the authority of the body over the mind, will we consent to remain under that sinful barrage? What would the Messiah do? It is unfathomable that He would opt to live in such a scene of immorality. Amy Carmichael once emphasized, "We cannot go for entanglements of any sort, and for spiritual power at the same time."[28] It is time to choose between the two.

Sodom's Costs Are Too Great

Admittedly, college does have attractive benefits, but not without costs that most often far outweigh those benefits. Family and friends may tell you, "You're strong enough to keep your faith through college; *you* won't become one of those statistics." But can a person be sure of that? Satan fell from heaven and Eve fell from the garden of Eden. Our hearts are deceitful, and they seek excuses to sin. "Therefore let him who thinks he stands take heed lest he fall," the Bible warns, in 1 Corinthians 10:12.

Some uphold Daniel and Joseph as examples of staying strong in college-like settings (Babylon and Egypt). They suggest that when you go to the university of Babylon, if you set your mind beforehand to be an overcomer, you will be victorious. The issue these people ignore in recommending this, however, is that Daniel and Joseph were dragged into those settings against their will—they were captives. The difference between them and us is that we have a *choice* of whether to put ourselves into such corrupting environments. Not only that, but we pay megabucks to be swept into the maelstrom, and simultaneously pray to overcome the very thing we purchase. If Daniel had had the option of going to Babylon to study under pagan education, he would have refused, and chosen to remain in Israel—guaranteed.

It is very hard to live in the midst of a Sodom-like setting and not join in the activities of those around us. As Reb Bradley put it, "You can't walk on the curb for a long time without stepping into the street."

If we truly believe that college often typifies Sodom, then longing for it could be as deadly as it was for Lot's wife when she looked back. Sodom, her home, was similar to college with all its attractions, stimulations, and ventures into the thrills of the world. She probably dreaded the dreary existence that faced her: living in a cave. It was when she doubted the value of her forthcoming life of hardship that she longed for the familiarity of the worldliness of Sodom—"the treasures of Egypt," so to speak. She looked back when she stopped looking ahead to her reward (see Hebrews 11).

We never fully know what great fallout hinges on our obedience. Perhaps it was more of a miracle that the rest of Lot's wife's family did *not* turn into a pillar of salt than that she *did*. Sulfur was pouring down from the heavens, likely petrifying every inhabitant of Sodom and Gomorrah into a pillar of salt, not just Lot's wife. Could it be that while Lot's family had their hearts set on obedience they were supernaturally protected, but when his wife allowed the desire of her fleshly nature to guide her feet, God's protection was removed?

Think how different the outcome could have been if Mrs. Lot had obeyed all the way, and stayed master of her heart, so that forgetting what was behind and straining toward what was ahead she would have pressed on toward the goal to win the prize for which God had called her (paraphrasing Philippians 3:13-14). Sure, she still would have met with a dingy cave and "lacked cultural stimulation" (as we ourselves might be tempted to complain), but her influence could have united her family toward pursuing godliness if she had so chosen.

Just her presence there would have saved them from the fruit of the calamitous strategizing of her daughters. Perhaps her motherly heart would have remembered the

318 mighty, godly men in Abraham's nearby household (see Genesis 14:14) as marriage potential for her daughters. History would have had a different outcome had she not longed for Sodom. Different human beings would exist. Different nations would have resulted. Her moment of choice decided it all. When she let her heart long for the self-fulfillment offered by the world (which colleges across the globe use as tantalizing bait today), she paid the price. Her choice affected her family and the history of the world.

According to m-w.com, a maelstrom is "a powerful, often violent, whirlpool sucking in objects within a given radius." So, perhaps it is time to remove ourselves from the reach of that radius, and to declare, "Where my God is not welcome, there I cannot abide." Paul exhorted Timothy, and by extension us, to "Flee also youthful lusts; but pursue righteousness, faith, love, peace with those who call on the Lord out of a pure heart" (2 Timothy 2:22).

3

ACADEMIC ASSAULT

"See to it that no one takes you captive through hollow and deceptive philosophy, which depends on human tradition and the elemental spiritual forces of this world rather than on Christ." (Colossians 2:8)

"The places that were formerly referred to as bastions of 'academic freedom' have become gulags of political correctness run amok."[1] So stated an article in "The College Illusion," an issue of *Whistleblower* magazine. How true. Instead of being places of intellectual sharpening where any idea can receive fair discussion, colleges today assault the minds of students through academics that more closely resemble indoctrination. Any idea that opposes the worldview of a professor has little chance of surviving unassailed in the classroom.

A college education used to involve learning how to think critically for oneself. Today, a degree only indicates that someone—motivated by fear of grade penalization—has learned to parrot back the exact information their professors wanted. As Jeff Shafer, a Christian lawyer, said in his speech about the "University of Babylon,"[2] "Education has become a systematic process of filtering opinions so students develop the 'right' view." Whoever holds the place of authority in the classroom somehow gets to determine what is right; everyone else will be mentally assaulted until they agree. What bothers Dallas Willard about this is that "the students are paying the salaries of the people who are doing that, which means they're paying to be abused!"[3]

Under the guise of academic scholarship, college professors have begun tearing down the authority of Scripture, teaching completely illogical views (such as postmodern relativism), proclaiming wrong to be right (such as by not condemning Hitler), and unashamedly delving deep into immoral topics.

Liberal Professors

The fact is that college faculties are disproportionately liberal. The percentage of liberal professors who teach at universities is far higher than the percentage of liberals in the general population. In 2003, the Center for the Study of Popular Culture conducted a study of thirty-two elite colleges, and found that of the faculties represented, "the overall ratio of registered Democrats to registered Republicans was more than 10 to 1."[4] Compare that to the rest of America's population, where closer to half of the people have conservative voter registrations. "The ratios themselves are impossible to understand in the absence of a political bias,"[5] states an article on the subject in "The College Illusion." The *Whistleblower* editor writes, "This is no trivial matter, and predictably results in the ongoing indoctrination—some critics even call it brainwashing—of millions of students."[6]

In any other setting, such a disproportionate percentage would be labeled "minority discrimination" for the sake of those students who are not fairly represented. But not so at college. There, administrations do not mind if the campus "creates a hostile environment for conservative students."[7] No wonder so many originally conservative young people vote liberally once they graduate. It is because "most students at these schools probably graduate without ever taking a class taught by a professor with a conservative viewpoint."[8] When immersed in such liberalism, one begins to think that the liberal way of thinking must be the only acceptable way.

Curriculum

Because most professors are liberal, college curriculum at public universities is obviously not taught from the cohesive perspective of a Christian worldview. Thus the curriculum "has no moral, social or intellectual center ... but [is rather] a meaningless hodgepodge of subjects."[9] Though college ought to be a time for emerging young adults to be able to seek the purpose of life, instead, "higher education ... more often than not excludes the deepest human questions—those of meaning and morality—from the curriculum."[10] College courses do not offer a biblical framework from which to process life; worse yet, *every subject* is leavened with the enemy's ideology.

Soft and Easy

Even in a worldly estimation, students no longer receive a thorough broad education through the college curriculum. In the article "Is College Really Worth It?" Phyllis Schlafly points out:

> Well-paid leftwing professors teach hundreds of so-called 'niche' courses that crowd out general knowledge and skills. [For example,] California State University at Monterey Bay allows students to count the History of Rock and Roll as their required course in U.S. History. Emory University allows students to choose among ... courses ... including one called Gynecology in the Ancient World. A class about television satisfies a Literature requirement at the University of Wisconsin at Madison. The University of California in Los Angeles offers Queer Musicology."[11]

This is now considered *higher* education?

Are hodgepodges of arbitrarily required college subjects actually teaching students anything valuable over the long run? Apparently not much. In the book *Academically Adrift*, "sociologists Richard Arum and Josipa Roksa report that 45 percent of college students hadn't significantly improved their critical thinking and writing skills after two years [of college]; after four years, the proportion was still 36 percent."[12] So, nearly half of all college students are not gaining the very thing college is supposed to give them—an education.

In fact, the literacy rate among college graduates has declined sharply over the last dozen years. Now only 29% of individuals who graduate from college have proficient reading skills, according to the National Assessment of Adult Literacy. This is appalling. College has failed at the job of education.

College courses are dumbed down to what used to be a high school level, so that students who do not excel in academics can pass. Yes, people who are not academically inclined go to college (trade schools would be a much better fit for many of them). They don't really belong in a university, but administrations want to falsely encourage them to continue their studies as long as possible in order to collect tuition from them. As Jim Nelson Black writes in his book, *Freefall of the American University*, "The cost of a college education has never been higher, and admissions standards have never been lower."[13] Therefore, classes become less rigorous as professors make assignments easier for incompetent students.

The attitude of our culture—"everyone deserves to succeed, regardless of whether their work has earned them the right"—contributes to professors' academic leniency. Janie Cheaney, in her *World Magazine* article, "Boastful Dunces," pointed out, "A-lower-than-expected grade [has become] not a wake-up call for diligence but an alarm that their fragile self-esteem has been breached."[14] To help students not wallow in low self-esteem, schools even label certain people "non-readers" and demand that their professors allow them to do alternative assignments, such as giving an oral report of a movie instead of writing a research paper.

As a result of not demanding academic rigor, the quality of a college education spirals downward. Rare young people who want to be challenged in college often admit that they find college easier than high school.

College Testimony from History: Edward Gibbon
(1737-1794), **historian and author of**
The Decline and Fall of the Roman Empire

"[My time at Oxford] proved 14 months of the most idle and unprofitable of my whole life..." [15]

—EDWARD GIBBON

Though students are not getting sharper, grade inflation masks the poor education they are actually receiving. In 2009, 43% of university grades were A's, compared to only 15% in 1960.[16] It used to be challenging to get an A in school; now it is almost a birthright. Paul Copperman, in his book, *The Literacy Hoax,* writes about this problem:

> "Grade inflation penalizes the superior, the talented, and the hard working, and rewards the mediocre, incompetent, and lazy. ... It teaches America's brightest young people that there is no particular merit attached to hard work. It is a measure of the deterioration of our institutions of higher education."[17]

And they *have* deteriorated. In the early eighties, the National Commission on Excellence in Education actually admitted, "If an unfriendly foreign power had attempted to impose on America the mediocre educational performance that exists today, we might well have viewed it as an act of war."[18]

In his article, "The Dangers of 'Higher Education,' " Thomas Sowell pointed out the sad truth that "too many of the people coming out of even our most prestigious academic institutions graduate with neither the skills to be economically productive nor the intellectual development to make them discerning citizens and voters."[19] Jim Nelson Black wrote, "High self-esteem and a blissful sense of accomplishment won't take graduates very far in a highly competitive marketplace, particularly when better educated men and women from Third World nations are vying for top jobs."[20]

"Western Civilization is Bad"

Not only are college courses letting up on the challenging academic education they used to provide, but they also are criticizing the very culture that once placed high value on the advancement of the mind through higher education—that is, Western civilization. Colleges are becoming platforms for socialist and even communist propaganda, as they condemn capitalism and the very choices that birthed America. As Jim Nelson Black wrote, "The university campus is no longer a center of higher learning but a socialist conspiracy that feeds on itself."[21]

The excellent film, *Agenda* (Copybook Heading Productions: 2010), dives into how the Communist Party USA met at the University of California, Berkeley in 1992, and outlined its agenda of cultural takeover. Its plan was to infiltrate academic institutions and change how people think—through evolution of thought rather than through revolution.

Communists on campus call themselves progressives. They do not go by the name of communism, so as to avoid any negative reactions. Their tactic is to promote socialism first, because people like the idea of the government solving all their problems. However, socialism is basically big government and there is no example in history of big government that didn't abuse its power over the people. Many do not realize that, as Vladimir Lenin said, "*The goal of socialism is communism.*" Socialism is only a dangerous stepping-stone.

Even though the twentieth century was the bloodiest of all due to communism—135 million people died because of it—dangerous communistic ideology still finds a forum from which to encroach upon citizens' liberties through college lectures. *Agenda* points out that most people under the age of fifty have no idea what it looks like to live under communism, therefore college campuses are perfect breeding grounds for communism's acceptance. Lenin himself stated, "Give me four years to teach the children and the seed I have sown will never be uprooted."

Specifically, the Harvard Graduate School of Education, for one, is set on dismantling Western civilization through subverting its significance. It has gotten so bad at Harvard that at a "conference on student research [they] featured a panel discussion on the topic 'Cuban Education: Our Role Model?' "[22] As Black wrote, "The ideal of today's campus radicals is to exchange a venerated history of liberty and justice for a discredited social nightmare."[23] Are we blind to the immense dangers of communistic government, or are its supportive professors intentionally dulling our senses to the threat?

In another instance, Yale could not bring itself to teach Western civilization, so it rejected a gift from a conservative donor of $20 million designated for that purpose.[24]

Students in many colleges, not just Harvard and Yale, are brainwashed through "thought evolution" to condemn everything that built Western civilization. Professors teach that:

- "Christianity is largely a history of inquisitions, crusades, oppression, and anti-intellectualism. Islam, on the other hand, is 'a religion of peace.' Therefore, criticism of Christianity is enlightened, while criticism of Islam is Islamophobia.
- "Mothers and fathers are interchangeable.
- "The great world and societal battles are not between good and evil, but between rich and poor and the powerful and the powerless.
- "The Constitution says what progressives think it should say.
- "Human beings are animals. They differ from 'other animals' primarily in having better brains.

- "The American dropping of the atom bomb on Hiroshima was an act of racism and a war crime."[25]

Usually, this assault against beliefs that a person would logically hold to on their own occurs through intimidating assumptions, rather than open debate of both sides. The college climate assumes that educated people believe there is no difference between a man and a woman, for example. If both sides were presented equally in a debate, students would be able to choose whether to believe such a position. As it stands, however, any student who dares to claim that Western civilization and capitalism are advantageous will be ridiculed.

Focusing on Darkness

At its zenith, should higher education really involve cramming obscure and depressing historical vignettes into students' minds in order for them to pass a test, so they can move on to the next topic that exalts another lowest common denominator? Dennis Prager describes the stance of liberal arts educators in his article, "What Kids Now Learn in College":

> There is no better and no worse in literature and the arts. The reason universities in the past taught Shakespeare, Michelangelo, and Bach rather than, let us say, Guatemalan poets, Sri Lankan musicians, and Native American storytellers was 'Eurocentrism.'[26]

Eurocentrism, in their jargon, is a focus on European culture and history to the exclusion of a wider view of the world. As we just discovered, universities are intent on diminishing the preeminence of Western civilization. Thus, they offer courses about oppressed minorities as a "superior" option to studying the classics and the U.S. Constitution, and Eurocentrism has become a derogatory term. As Black states, "Chaucer, Dante, Milton, Shakespeare, Tolstoy, Melville, and Twain [are] out, and any writer with a racial, sexual, or political ax to grind [is] suddenly in."[27]

Is this an expanding education—to wallow in mucky literature and become well versed in the downfalls of humanity, but not to study and become inspired by the culture-enriching periods of history? When a curriculum lauds depravity, students' natural response is to personally aspire to nothing better. Therefore, liberal arts studies at college can directly lead to increased immorality, victimized behavior, depression, and suicide, rather than the uplifting inspiration one might expect from higher education.

"Immorality Equals Academics"

Nearly every subject has become a platform for immoral godlessness at the university. History, English literature, art, music, and the sciences—all are corrupted nowadays by tentacles of immorality.

Art: It is tough, if not impossible, to avoid immorality when immersed in a college art department. "Professors refuse to draw the line between pornography and art,"[28] pointed out the author of *Brainwashed: How Universities Indoctrinate America's Youth*. Those who wish to study art in college have a tough time avoiding the study of nude models. Even some Christian colleges support such modeling, with the excuse that humans were the crowning glory of creation. Never mind the fact that God clothed mankind after the Genesis Fall, and that it has been a shameful thing to be naked in public ever since.

When God brought about the humiliation of Babylon, He metaphorically warned them that nakedness would be part of their judgment: " 'Your nakedness shall be uncovered, yes, your shame will be seen' " (Isaiah 47:3). The demon possessed man who came out of the caves to see the Messiah was naked. Therefore, the scriptural pattern is clear, as Jeff Pollard stated in *Christian Modesty and the Public Undressing of America*:

> God's people *cover* their bodies in public, while pagans often *uncover* theirs. ... God covered man in the Garden; it appears that Satan and the devils have been trying to strip him ever since.[29]

Therefore, it would seem that nude modeling is never acceptable in the Creator's sight, even for the sake of art.

English is another especially risky subject for believers to study at college. Much of the required literature continually features immorality. Such books certainly do not pass the Philippians 4:8 test:

> Whatever things are true, whatever things are noble, whatever things are just, whatever things are pure, whatever things are lovely, whatever things are of good report, if there is any virtue and if there is anything praiseworthy—meditate on these things.

When reading almost any English literature requirement it is nearly impossible to obey this Scripture. Of course, many wholesome books exist that could be studied, but instead, liberal professors are notorious for choosing downright wicked literature.

Science: In the sciences, new ventures into biotechnology (manipulations with human life) challenge biblical ethics at every step. Is it right to delve into studying cloning techniques, embryonic stem cell research, or transforming human zygotes into animals, for example? Deliberating the ethics of the idea should be the foundation of each of these forays; however, modern science does not care what God has to say about the morality of experiments. Thus the studies continue, from college onward.

Bioethical dilemmas extend on into medical school due to the fact that abortion is often a part of medical training. Usually universities do not make it known whether or not performing an abortion will be a graduation requirement until a student's junior year. Then, when "the med student's career is at stake ... a strong inducement [exists] for him to give up his principles to fulfill the requirements for success in his chosen field."[30]

Even in subjects where it seems impossible for moral muck to invade or for questionable ethics to triumph, some professors find a way. For example, I registered for a course in Economics, thinking that that topic would surely be void of immoral content. However, it was not. We students ended up enduring an undisciplined 300-400 pound professor tell us about his lust life and drinking habits when he was in college. All the girls in the class were petrified to go alone to his office to turn in their assignments. I learned less economic theory in that college course than I did in high school, because of time he wasted on immoral ranting.

A class can only rise to as high a standard as the professor possesses. Since the majority of professors are extreme liberals with wicked appetites and little sense of right and wrong, academics at college tend to be heavily tainted with immorality. Such courses are totally unsuited for any believer to have to endure. Academic assault has subverted higher education.

Relativism

"Everything's relative" is the cry of professors from classroom to classroom. They ask, "What does this book mean to *you?*" rather than, "What did the *author* mean by this?" Then they conclude that whatever the book means to you is what it means, period; no objective reality exists.

Really? Do professors themselves believe this? What if someone read an article *they* wrote, and claimed it meant something different because of how the reader felt about the topic? Of course, the professor who authored it would not take kindly to relativism *then*. But, many times teachers are blind to the illogic of relativism, even when a student pointedly answers the absurd "everything's relative" declaration with the probing question: "Is *that* relative?" Professors want to claim that the statement "everything's relative" is *not* relative *itself*, but rather an objective, solid truth claim. But that is an illogical position.

No one can live in a way that is consistent with believing everything is relative. When a waiter brings a customer something he did not order, he does not just accept it, saying, "everything's relative, so it's fine that when I ordered 'lasagna' that meant 'sandwich' to you." Of course not! We demand the exact thing that we ordered, because words have concrete *objective* meaning, not variable *relative* meaning.

If there is no objective meaning to life—that is, meaning that exists whether or not we agree with it—then what is the point of grades? If there is no objective standard of excellent scholarship then grading is pointless. Professors' actions are inconsistent with their belief in relativism, because they still grade papers.

An education based on relativism is nonsensical. Nevertheless, professors teach relativism and cling to it, because if "everything's relative," then there is no God, and sin exists only by each person's definition of it (if it exists at all). Then the professor can live in whatever way he or she wants, because "everything's relative."

In response to this failure of academicism, 1 Corinthians 3:19-20 alerts:

> For the wisdom of this world is foolishness with God. For it is written, "He catches the wise in their own craftiness;" and again, "The LORD knows the thoughts of the wise, that they are futile."

Toying around with clever philosophic arguments in order to avoid truth is futile. Wisdom that is not founded upon truth is foolish, not the other way around

Criticism of Scripture

Even courses on the Bible may have dangers lurking within. Professors pride themselves in teaching Scripture from an "academic" point of view, and this often means they discredit the validity of the Word of God. Academic criticism of Scripture causes doubt to take the place of belief, as obscure superficial contradictions within the Bible are one-sidedly presented. The more of these a professor can point out, the more certain he is of shaking students' confidence in the authority of the Bible.

As Doug Phillips so eloquently stated in *The Mysterious Islands* film (Erwin Brothers, 2009), "Compromise of authority of Scripture leads to skepticism, which leads to disbelief. Disbelief leads to open hostility toward the God of Scripture." Thus, tearing down the authority of Scripture ultimately leads to hostility toward God. It is impossible to trust in the God of the Bible while believing that the Book He inspired is in error.

There are many, many lines of assault that Bible professors use to discredit the validity of Scripture, including: the JEDP theory (Moses did not write the Torah; it was written by at least four different authors), the "two" creation accounts (Genesis 1-2 contradict each other), theistic evolution (creation did not occur in six days, but rather during millions of years), and numerous smaller points of contention. Let's take a closer look at some of these academic criticisms of Scripture.

> Academic "criticism in the universities,
> I'll have to admit, has entered a phase
> where ... it's Stalinism without Stalin."[31]
> —HAROLD BLOOM, professor at Yale University

"Pentateuch Not Written by Moses"

When I found my college roommate reading Genesis one day, I was rather excited. She had to read the whole book through in just a few days for her Introduction to the Old Testament class. I had never seen her reading her Bible before, so I thought it was a great development. That is, until I heard about a usurper nicknamed JEDP who insinuated to her that Genesis could not be trusted.

The JEDP theory claims that Moses did not write the Torah after all, but four people or groups of people authored it instead. In developing this theory, liberal Christian scholars labeled the numerous authors as:

- **J** for the author that used the name Jehovah (Yahweh) for God
- **E** for the author that used the name Elohim for God
- **D** for the author of Deuteronomy
- **P** for the author of the priestly sections

I was shaken to hear about JEDP. If Moses didn't actually write the Torah, how could I know for sure that Paul wrote Corinthians or John penned Revelation? If different authors dreamed up those books years after the events occurred, the Bible would topple off its throne of authority in my soul!

So my excitement to see my roommate reading her Bible waned as she tentatively shared how she wasn't sure if her faith could ever be the same. My roommate emphatically warned me to never take the course she was enduring. That was a difficult challenge, however, since that course and others like it were required to graduate. (I ended up avoiding the assault by chucking college.)

From where did this specific defiance of scriptural authority originate? Since seminaries teach this theory as fact, we might assume that some confused Christian scholar dreamed it up. But no, the fact is that a pantheist named Baruch de Spinoza came up with it in 1670, and was excommunicated from his Jewish community and condemned by Christians as a result.[32]

If that weren't reason enough to denounce the theory, ten times the Old Testament writers from Joshua to Malachi stated in passing that Moses was the author of the Torah, by calling it "the law of Moses." This is further confirmed fourteen times in the Gospels and Epistles— some of those instances by the Messiah Himself (such as Mark 12:26). Are seminary professors claiming that they know who authored the Torah and the Savior does not?

Professors argue that Moses would not have been educated enough to write the Pentateuch that early in world history, but this is not sufficiently convincing either, because plenty of Egyptian records exist which date from the time of Moses and even before.

Also, none of the ancient Torah manuscripts supply evidence for the JEDP multi-author hypothesis. Moses probably included some small portions from oral tradition (such as the account of the flood and the history of Abraham's life), but this does not necessarily diminish the authenticity of Moses' authorship. Likewise, Moses' obituary at the end of Deuteronomy does not negate his having written the rest of the Torah. It is not unusual for someone else to add a postscript to a book after the author's death (in this case, Joshua probably wrote it).

We can find encouragement from the excellent appendix that addresses this topic in the book *Already Compromised*:

> Christians who believe Moses wrote the Pentateuch do not need to feel intellectually intimidated. It is the enemies of the truth of God that are failing to think carefully and face the facts honestly. ... The attack on the Mosaic authorship of the Pentateuch is nothing less than an attack on the veracity, reliability, and authority of the Word of Almighty God.[33]

So, I need not have allowed the JEDP theory to challenge the authority of the Bible in my life, but few college campuses would admit that, and few Christian college students know how to answer the theory. Which is just what their professors hope.

"Two Creation Accounts"

Another common academic criticism of Scripture revolves around Genesis 1-2. Many professors teach this passage as a poetic myth because the two creation accounts are "completely out of sync with each other," and they "contradict each other because the order of creation in both chapters is different." They argue that Genesis 2 shows that man was created *before* plants and animals, while Genesis 1 states the opposite. They base this on the order of the verses in Genesis 2:

1. Genesis 2:7: "The Lord God formed *man* of the dust of the ground"
2. Genesis 2:9: "And out of the ground the Lord God made every *tree*"
3. Genesis 2:19: "Out of the ground the Lord God formed every *beast* of the field and every bird of the air"

Contrasted to this, the creation order of Genesis 1 is:

1. Genesis 1:11-13: plants
2. Genesis 1:24-25: animals
3. Genesis 1:26-27: man

Professors love to present this as a contradiction, and then let students sweat in their seats as they try to find an answer that upholds the inerrancy of Scripture. Of course, it is very difficult to think of answers under pressure, and most Christian students have never thought of this dilemma before college. Even if a student vocalizes a good comeback right then, it will often be belittled because of the forceful authority of the professor's opposing assertion.

To invalidate this "contradiction," it is necessary to realize that Genesis 2 offers a poetic retelling of creation that is not intended to be chronological. Genesis 1 provides the sequential record, while Genesis 2 zooms in to focus on the details of the sixth day of creation. Moses tells the story of Adam in Genesis 2 and, in order to do so, he pulls in different parts of creation at the point where they fit into Adam's story (e.g. stating that God formed every beast before saying that Adam named them, but after telling about Adam's creation). In a way, the literary style of chapter two mimics a lady talking about what she did on a certain day: "I went to the store [afternoon], and I had a phone call from Sally [mid morning], and I cooked dinner [just now]." We don't think it deceitful of her to tell the events of her day out of order, because we understand that the chronology is not important.

Another way to solve the discrepancy is to understand that in Genesis 2:9 and 19 (printed above), the verb "made" or "formed" could be translated "had made/had formed." In fact, Tyndale's translation (which predates the KJV) does translate it this way, as does the NIV. But even without the translation "had formed," Genesis 2 never states that animals were created after man (by stating, "*then* God formed every beast").

This small deceptive teaching has robbed more students of their faith than it is comfortable to comprehend. The enemy knows that if he can destroy a person's confidence in the first two chapters of the Bible, he or she will then have little reason to trust the validity of the rest of it.[*]

---

[*] Christian Apologetics and Research Ministry: www.CARM.org offers helpful insight into resolving other "contradictions."

Evolution

Whether a student majors in the sciences or merely takes a single required biology class, evolution crouches as a tiger ready to take down students who might dare to believe the literal, historical account of Genesis. Some might think there is no problem with believing in evolution as a Christian. However, the belief that God initiated evolution and then allowed creation week to extend for eons of years implies that death occurred before the Fall of mankind (if animals evolved and died in the process to make way for higher forms of life). This would mean that the Creator called death "very good," since He made that pronouncement at the end of creation week.

It follows that if death was not a *punishment* for sin, but rather a *natural process* of evolution, then the Savior's death was meaningless. Perhaps that logic is the very point of evolutionism—to declare that sin is inconsequential, therefore people need not fear eternal punishment for it. If death is not the consequence of sin, then we are not responsible to a Creator for our actions, and we can act like unprincipled animals—which is all we are, according to evolutionary theory ("from goo to you, by way of the zoo!").

Therefore, is it really logical for a Christian to believe in evolution if the very essence and reason underlying the evolutionary theory is to avoid the need for the Savior? As Geoffrey Bull, a believer who was imprisoned for his faith in China, stated in his moving book, *God Holds the Key*, "Intellectualism that crucifies the Son of God afresh and puts Him to an open shame will meet the fate that it deserves."[34] Answers in Genesis, a ministry actively devoted to proclaiming the veracity of Genesis 1-11, stands firm in the conviction that it is not consistent for a Christian to believe in evolution.

Aside from being an affront to salvation, evolution also defies logic by its lack of evidence. There is no scientific need to choose evolution over creation, nor is it more academically valid. While evolutionists lack fossil-record proof of transitional forms, Bible believers see plenty of evidence of the veracity of Genesis 1-11 (marine animal fossils atop mountains proving the flood, the shallow depth of dust on the moon proving the universe is young, etc.).

Yet colleges—public, private, and Christian—teach evolution as fact in their science departments. A visit to the bookstore at Wheaton College, for example, will shock a Bible-believing creationist, due to the plethora of theistic evolutionary books on the shelves. Christian universities usually present the biblical creation account as largely (if not completely) figurative, and definitely unreliable.

Public universities do not even try to explain away the creation account in their science courses, but rather sneer at it as an uneducated myth. Evolutionary biologist Kenneth Miller revealed how faith is treated in many public academic settings:

> A presumption of atheism or agnosticism is universal in academic life. [It] revolve[s] around the assumption that religious belief is something that people grow out of as they become educated.[35]

This is the root of the danger for Christian students' faith. Evolutionary professors declare that only uneducated people believe in a Creator God. Many students succumb to this intimidation and allow themselves to become "educated" by abandoning their faith in the Creator and the way His Word says the world began.

David Kupelian describes evolution as "the eternal dance of purposeless recombination of ever-more-complex forms, but all without meaning, without spirit, without love." Evolution is a convenient theory for avoiding the answer to why we are here: to glorify God and enjoy Him forever (as the Westminster Catechism states). Believing in evolution allows one to live for self, to declare that sin is relative, and to ignore one's ultimate accountability to the Judge of all the earth. This debate runs far deeper than the level of science.

Dangerous Incubation!

The danger of most collegiate textual criticism that is aimed at eroding students' faith in Scripture is that a student thinks, "I don't really believe that, but I'll store it away in my mind to study *why* I don't believe it later, when I have time." The problem is, "later" is often an entire nine months later, when summer finally arrives. College assignments are so absorbing that there is very little extra time; consequently, false assumptions are allowed to germinate in the mind for the length of a pregnancy. Because of the power of unchallenged assumptions, by the end of the school term students find themselves holding opinions they did not personally believe before, nor did they ever agree to.

Thus, some liberal professors knowingly or unknowingly lead impressionable students astray through unfounded textual criticism of Scripture. The clout of a professor with a PhD can intimidate students from standing for their beliefs. Doubts of the legitimacy of one's own thoughts compared to those of their highly educated teachers hold considerable sway over the mind. Even in spite of one's own solid beliefs, doubts creep in as to whether or not they are *educated* beliefs. Thoughts such as, "What right do I have to question this professor? He has a PhD in theology, and I am only a young adult," lead to the devastating conclusion, "Well, maybe it *is* a more educated position to believe that the Bible is not inspired, and that it is only a moral guide—the equivalent of other holy books."

College Testimony: Firing Heretical Professors

"Twenty years ago, I went to the only Christian university in the state, hoping for a solid, biblical education. Instead I spent time informing the administration and board members about the heresies being taught in the classroom. I knew the professors had signed a statement attesting to the inerrancy of Scripture when they were hired, so when I heard them teaching that Jonah was not historical and that theistic evolution was the only way to fit in science with biblical "stories," it bothered me. My parents had insisted I attend Summit Ministries before college. Because of the tools they gave me, I was willing and able to defend my faith in the classroom, but I witnessed too many other Christian kids start questioning the very foundation of their faith—the Word of God—and abandon it altogether within a couple of years.

So, I started recording what was being said in the classroom and reporting that evidence to the University board. As a result, three professors were fired while I was there, several more were under strict review and at least two more were fired or left because of the pressure placed on them in the following year."

—DORA FAUTH, homemaking wife and mother of six

Satan hurled Bible verses at the Messiah. It is possible to use the Word of God to do the opposite of what God intended.

Geoffrey Bull wrote about how we, as believers, ideally study Scripture: "We shift from analyzing the Bible to *it* analyzing *us*."[36] This is the esteem in which we should hold the Word of God, even in academic study.

Conclusion

Matthew 22:37 calls God's people to "Love the Lord your God with all your heart and with all your soul and with all your *mind*." Do college academics help us obey this greatest command of the One Who created us? How can we aptly love the Lord with our minds, when our minds are filled with immoral thoughts, liberal professors' agendas, and doubts about the validity of Scripture?

Biblical apologist and science educator Christopher Ashcraft thinks that "unfortunately, as Christians we too quickly become of the world and start doing things the way of the secular culture. And that is also the case with education. We have adopted the purpose of education as defined by our society." Our society encourages young people to attend college in order to gain worldly knowledge, indulge in immoral experimentation, and eventually acquire material wealth as a result of having a degree. But the wisest man in the world told us, "There is no wisdom or understanding or counsel against the Lord" (Proverbs 21:30). Any education that runs in contrary channels to the Lord's highest pathways is not worth our investment of time, thought, and money.

Even if a student is fortunate enough to be able to study uplifting topics and literature at college, the classroom model is not the ultimate way to learn. Rushing to complete a book in order to pass a test results in nowhere near as thorough an education as being able to soak in the material and ask questions in order to understand what the author is getting at, and then analyze his or her conclusions. Superficially breezing through books causes many people to never want to read again after college. Who wants to be unable to evaluate what they are reading because of pressure to finish a book? Or who wants to be required to read a book they completely disagree with or don't have any interest in? The pressured study habits of college often do not generate lifetime lovers of learning.

Unhelpful College Habit #3: Stress

College cultivates a lifestyle of stress. From morning till night, students run from one class to the next, hurriedly attempting to finish assignments just in time, and cramming for exams. Financially strapped students who attempt to work a job while studying full-time become especially stressed. Honestly, does any other four-year period of life occasion so much needless intense stress? Nobody is dying, and class assignments are really not as important as other things in life.

The college environment conditions people to respond stressfully to demands, a chronic habit which can continue long after college. On the contrary, productivity at home is instinctively best accomplished with measured tread.

College can become a "snare of preparation" that holds one back from living. Jane Addams wrote about this phrase of Tolstoy's:

> We spread [the snare of preparation] before the feet of young people, hopelessly entangling them in a curious inactivity at the very period of life when they are longing to construct the world anew and to conform it to their own ideals.[37]

For motivated students, college may be an obstacle that delays them from accomplishing their goals. For young people who do not have vision for what they should do with their lives, college is often a means of escape. Majors in anthropology, English, or philosophy, for example, can be a postponement of reality, and students working towards these types of degrees often get stuck in academia. They don't know what to do with themselves outside of college, so they return again and again for more degrees and debt.

College is not an end-all-be-all destination. People have inherent worth without its stamp of approval. In his article, "The Disadvantages of an Elite Education," William Deresiewicz wrote:

> An elite education inculcates a false sense of self-worth … You learn to think of yourself in terms of numbers [SAT, GPA, GRE]. They come to signify not only your fate, but your identity; not only your identity, but your value. … One of the great errors of an elite education, then, is that it teaches you to think that measures of intelligence and academic achievement are measures of value in some moral or metaphysical sense. But they're not. Graduates of elite schools are not more valuable than stupid people, or talentless people, or even lazy people. Their pain does not hurt more. Their souls do not weigh more.[38]

No, the point of education should not be to study wickedness, nor to race through books just to be done with them, nor to avoid facing the mission of life through becoming a perpetual college student, nor to only feel complete once awarded a diploma. Education of the mind should rather be for the purpose of equipping us with adept ability to respond to life's challenges as dominion-takers and cultivators of excellence, made in the image of the righteous, pure, and orderly God of the universe.

Indeed, it is vital to pursue education, but true education is not something graded by tests and finalized by age twenty-two. Education is a lifelong process of disciplining and stretching one's mental acuity, and it is a process that we go after ourselves. A well-educated person does not reach that level by being spoon-fed. Having influential wise counsel to shape the advanced education we independently pursue is invaluable, but we must remember that others don't give us an education. The path of education begins with our own will and grit of mental discipline.

Ultimately, worship of God ought to be the end goal of education. If worship is not possible through college academics, perhaps college is not the best avenue for a believer to take.

For it is written: "I will destroy the wisdom of the wise, and bring to nothing the understanding of the prudent." Where is the wise? Where is the scribe? Where is the disputer of this age? Has not God made foolish the wisdom of this world? … the world through wisdom did not know God. (1 Corinthians 1:19-21)

Only the world thinks its academics are wise. God thinks otherwise and can guide us each to wise academic education that recognizes Him as its ultimate end.

Chucking College Testimony: Dropped in, Not out

"I went to college for three years, studying art and agriculture. One day, a book in the college library triggered me to think more about the ideologies behind the academic model of college.

University academia is a tradition rooted in Greek intellectual culture and religion. I noted the connection between the first college—Plato's academy—and the rites of Dionysus/Bacchus, the Greek god of theatre, wine, and revelry. Sounded just like modern college to me! I had tried to weed the Greek way of thinking out of my spiritual life in favor of a more holistic Hebrew perspective,* yet I realized I was voting with my dollars and my presence at college for the survival of the very things I wanted to uproot.

My experience was that college life fostered a disconnected and hurried lifestyle because of the habits it was necessary to adopt to succeed there. College promoted (even celebrated) caffeine dependence and all-night work sessions, and caused me to neglect creative excellence because of the sheer number of projects due at the same time. I realized four or more years of these habits would be hard to shake off when it came time to live a more centered and healthy life.

---

* The Greek educational model involves acquiring theoretical mental information, while the more biblical Hebrew model is based on discipleship and life integration of content.

These factors and more brought me to realize that college was not putting me on a trajectory to my real goals (nor was it matching my values), and if I wanted an authentic education I would have to look for it elsewhere on my own. I realized that for less than the price of one college art course, I could drive to another city and take a personal weekend seminar from my favorite Christian painter, and then go home and apply what I learned on my own projects instead of spending time on assignments that did not significantly further my own aspirations. Or I could even take a college class here and there on a specifically interesting topic.

I wanted to be successful on God's and my terms, not the world's. I had to make a decision as to whether I was going to jump through the world's hoops so as to find opportunity there, or trust that God had a plan and a job for me to do and that He would arrange things accordingly. So I left college, and guess what? He did. I'm now doing graphic design work I care intensely about, on an international level, and no one cares that I don't have a degree. I've had my work published in major international news magazines and websites, and have designed book covers for published books (including the one in your hands).

I am so thankful that I left when I did. It didn't take long for me to get over the self-imposed shame of being a dropout and realize that I was dropping *in* to a much broader, more challenging and rewarding divinely appointed educational experience made just for me!"

—ERIN JONES (31), graphic designer

4

FINANCIAL FREEFALL

"The younger son gathered everything together and went on a journey into a distant country, and there he squandered his estate with loose living."
(Luke 15:13)

Though the biblical principle regarding debt is to owe no man anything (Romans 13:8), somehow we become easily convinced that a college degree is worth enough to sidestep that guideline. For it, people end up signing on to pay far more than they dreamed, to obtain a far poorer education than they expected.

Imagine if you had $50,000-$100,000 cash and could invest it in a way that would establish a solid foundation and launching pad for your adult life. Would you choose to spend it on attending required classes based on someone else's agenda for your life, on studying under liberal professors, on living with an arbitrarily assigned person, and on having your innocence and purity robbed?

Wouldn't you rather intentionally invest those valued savings on online courses and two-day workshops on subjects that specifically ignite and equip your unique talents and aptitudes? With that kind of money, perhaps you would choose to travel the world and acquire invaluable cultural exposure. Maybe you would choose to apprentice under a master in a certain field to sharpen your skills. Or you might dive right into launching a business with a portion of that capital (and purchase a fixer-upper, debt-free home with the remaining cash). In other words, wouldn't you want to invest such an inheritance in a way that would allow you to enter adult life with tools and solidarity, rather than debt and lost years with little to show for them?

Most of us do not have $100,000 of discretionary money to spend. So, we should be that much *more* careful not to misuse what we do have, nor to go into exorbitant debt for a degree that is beyond our means and of dubious value anyway. Without external pressure, few of us would agree to sign on for such a debilitating debt load in exchange for so little.

And yet, millions have done just that. Two thirds of students graduate college with an average debt load of $24,000 on their shoulders.[1] In fact, college debt usually ends up being more than students anticipate because "the total price usually quoted for college is the annual price times four. But that figure is grossly understated because only 60 percent of college students in four-year colleges graduate within six years."[2] In other words, to get an accurate idea of the debt trap college might spring on a student unaware, he or she should multiply the yearly tuition times *six* years.

With the interest of student loans factored in, it becomes clear that a college degree may end up costing twice as much as anticipated. Take a reasonable estimate of $100,000 of debt for four years at a private college (but remember, it takes 40% of students longer than six years to graduate). If, after a student with that amount of debt graduates, she can afford to pay $730 a month towards her student loan, at 7% interest it will take her 23 years to pay off that debt, and she will end up paying a total of $201,000 for that degree.

Think that is high? Okay, let's look at a less expensive college degree from a public university—"just" $42,000 for four years. After 23 years of laying down $300 a month, a graduate will still pay double: $84,000. These low-end estimates do not include hidden fees, penalties, and deceptive rate changes to double-digit interest, which many student loan companies fraudulently charge.

Due to compound interest—where interest is charged not only on the principal but also on the interest—after many years of faithfully paying each payment, a graduate could potentially owe more than the original debt, as this person testified:

> I am currently a public school teacher with an income of $50,000, barely enough income to pay the interest-only payments [of my student loans]. I have never missed a payment in over ten years ... and my loan balance stands

at $105,000. To date, I have paid over $40,000 in loan payments and because my income restricts me to interest-only payments, and the 7% daily capitalized interest rate, I now owe $15,000 more than I borrowed.[3]

Of course, she could pay off her loan faster by actively paying more each month (the longer time taken to pay off the debt, the more interest accrues), but few can afford to set aside $1,000 a month when they have not been able to secure a good job, or when they are starting up a new family and buying a home.

In fact, after leaving college, only one in five graduates can afford basic life necessities because of their debt load, according to a June 2012 survey.[4] The truth is, every individual who has student loan debt also faces an additional average of $12,000 in consumer debt—also accrued while at college (such as on a credit card). This means that the graduate who leaves college with debt does not face just the $25,000 tuition load, but they bear a total debt load of closer to $40,000. Therefore, in figuring the cost of college, all of the following should be taken into account: tuition, interest on student loans, interest on credit card debt, and lost income from years of not working while in college (even a modest annual income of $20,000 for four years adds up to quite a nice nest egg of $80,000).

American students as a whole have taken on so much debt that in late 2011 the national student debt balance topped $1 trillion and surpassed all credit card debt or car debt.[5] (To fathom the enormity of a trillion dollars, imagine that a company lost a million dollars a day, every day, from the time of Christ until now. Even at that rate, the business would not yet have lost a trillion dollars.)

The seemingly insurmountable debt burden of college makes many young people suicidal and hopeless rather than excited about flourishing in their future vocations. As Proverbs states, "The borrower becomes the lender's slave" (Proverbs 22:7). Debt rules a person's life, causing them to make decisions they might not make if they were not under the burden of creditors (such as delaying having children, or having to stick with an hourly wage job instead of becoming entrepreneurial, etc.). All of the preceding generations faced manageable college costs. Just a few decades ago, it was easily possible to pay for college with income from a summer job. Our culture has not yet seen the effects of the burden which $25,000-200,000 of debt lays upon a person.

> **"Student:** Why should I go to college?
> **Guidance Counselor:** So you can get a degree.
> **Student:** Why?
> **Counselor:** So you can get a good job.
> **Student:** Why?
> **Counselor:** So you can make more money.
> **Student:** Why?
> **Counselor:** So you can pay back your college loans."[6]
> —GARY VARVEL cartoon

There is virtually no way to escape student loan debt through bankruptcy, due to a 2005 revision to federal bankruptcy law. Defaulting on student loans is not a solution either. The government is determined to get their loans paid back, and they will do it through keeping graduates' tax refunds, garnishing their paychecks, or even suing them if they default. Also, employers do not prefer to hire people who have a loan default on their record.

College Testimony: The Burden of Student Loans

"I am 30 years old, and my wife is 28. Altogether, we are $185,000 in debt to the government for our educations. Paying off this debt will be our lives' work. We have an aggressive plan to tackle this monster, but it will be a full decade before we defeat it. There will be no dinners out, and very few fun things for most of the next 10 years until the debt is gone. Oh, and that law degree? It's not very valuable. It took my wonderful wife, who is quite brilliant, 18 months to find full-time employment. Her new job is also 150 miles away, and requires commuting there most of the week. Higher education is a scam!

I love my wife very much, and God elected her before the beginning of time to be His child, and to be my wife. But if I could have met her five years ago, and rescued her from the idea of investing in a career that precludes having children or a family for a decade

---

or more, we would be much better off. We would have only my university debt to pay off.

The student loan bubble will burst. And it will burst on the backs of young families just trying to survive. While a four-year degree used to be a legitimate signaling device to an employer that you were an educated person, now it is not. It simply means you know how to borrow money to buy a college degree.

For those deciding whether to take on student loans, please consider the following: You cannot walk away from it. I call college debt my mortgage without a house. Unlike a house, which you could simply move out of, if you cannot make the payments, there are no ways to get out of it. You must pay it back. There are no bankruptcies. You are their slave.

No other industry has so little consumer protection. Even a car loan puts the consumer in a better bargaining position than student loans–you can always sell the car.

But you say: 'After I get a degree, I will make more money!' That's not necessarily true. With a deflating economy and an inflating currency, you may actually come out worse. Your education is a potential risk, not just an investment."

—S. John (30), husband and college graduate

(reprinted with permission from: www.survivalblog.com/ 2011/07/a_prepper_goes_to_college_by_s.html)

As a desperate woman commented on an online news article about student loans, "If I could go back in time, I would not have [made the] ill-fated decision to take on student loan debt. Hindsight is 20/20. Ten years in prison would have been of greater benefit."

For many, their student loan burden will not be lifted until they die. Some feel prone to give up even trying to pay off their debt—yet year after year many more eighteen-year-olds enter college with no idea of the nightmare that student loan debt will bring.

Colleges are Businesses

It has not yet dawned on most of us that colleges are industries that aim to make a profit, just like any other business. Admissions counselors are simply college salesmen. They are not even college *degree* salesmen; they are only concerned with continued enrollment—which means that students get the short end of this business deal. If a student is in college for six years and then fails to graduate, administrations will not be concerned, because the longer that students are enrolled, the more income the college generates.

The admissions "salesmen" court prospective students by means of swanky envelopes (some complete with printed satiny ribbons or embossing) arriving day after day in the mail. They announce, "You've been accepted!" as if it is a rare honor. They deliver your latest scholarship award with little mention of how much is left to pay after the scholarship. The posh full-color brochures and letters signed by the dean are designed to carry applicants away from logic to elitist emotion. It is unrealistic, however, to deceive ourselves into thinking that they really want *us* that much. They do not really long for our brilliance or personality to grace their campus, but for our money to stuff their budget.

The same fiscal motivation lies behind the swanky edifice that campuses present—brick buildings, immaculate green lawns, multi-million dollar fitness centers and student unions, etc. How many parents express their pleasure over the college they want their child to attend because "It's a beautiful campus!" In actuality, the first class aesthetics of campus grounds are no measure of the quality of education inside. The fine packaging often conceals a disappointing product.

> "While students write poorly, professors prattle instead of teach. Meanwhile, parents pay tuition because it's socially the thing to do."[7]
> —MARVIN OLASKY, *World Magazine*

In the last twenty-five years, tuitions have increased four times faster than inflation. This means the cost of a college education is not rising proportionately to the rest of the economy. If any other societal good went up 400% in price, we would begin questioning the worth of it; college should not be an exception. Tuition has more than doubled since the 1980's,[8] and at the top schools in America, tuition is exorbitant. In the 2011-2012 school year, tuition cost with room and board for one year was:

$51,424 at Duke, $51,000 at Harvard, $50,012 at Yale, and $49,997 at Stanford.[9] Are we out of our minds? Multiply one of those tuitions by six years and the result is $300,000. For what? A ticket to prestige?

> "The fixation on college-going ... spawns the delusion that only the degree—not the skills and knowledge behind it—matters. We need to rethink."[10]
>
> —ROBERT J. SAMUELSON, *The Washington Post*

But People with Degrees Earn More

"In a lifetime, college graduates earn $1 million more than high school graduates." Or so we've been told. However, some are calling this the "million-dollar misunderstanding"[11] for several reasons. The main reason is that bright, motivated people are more apt to attend college in the first place than unmotivated ones, so they would likely make more money over a lifetime even without a degree. An article in *World Magazine* confirmed this: "Richard Vedder, an education economic expert, estimates that two-thirds of superior earning comes from the intelligence and character of the earner rather than the degree itself."[12]

Another reason that graduates might not actually make more than those who do not go to college is that the cost of obtaining a degree lingers with graduates for years and years after college. If Jessica is able to make $50,000 a year after graduating but has to pay $20,000 that year for her loans, she will not feel richer than Ashley who earns $30,000 a year without debt. Thus when what graduates owe is taken into account, for years they don't even catch up with someone who did not go into debt to get a degree. By the time they pay off their debt and their annual income does surpass the non-graduate's, it may be thirty-three years into their career, according to an article in *Forbes Magazine*.[13] That's for the fortunate ones who actually are able to pay off their debt. For medical professionals, some do not even anticipate being able to unless they win the lottery, because of their additional insurance and start-up equipment costs.

In this day and age, the presumption that people with degrees will be paid more is not as true as it was in the past. Since nearly everyone goes to college now, a degree no longer provides job seekers with as much differentiation in the workplace as it used to. Many with degrees cannot find jobs, but even if they can, their college loans consume their earnings. Doing the simple math reveals that financially, one would be better off with *any* job, even minimum wage, or a small home business, than to face seemingly insurmountable figures of debt with the highest-paying job around. Four to eight years of saving money, living at home, and being entrepreneurially productive have proven to advance some far beyond their friends who chose the college route. After all, a plumber without a degree earns more over a lifetime than a doctor or a lawyer (when educational loans are subtracted from their lifetime income).

19 High-paying Jobs Without a College Degree[14]

1. Air traffic controller: annual income: $102,030
2. Storage and distribution manager: $66,600
3. Transportation manager: $66,600
4. Police and detective supervisor: $64,430
5. Non-retail sales manager: $59,300
6. Forest fire fighting supervisor: $58,920
7. Municipal fire fighting supervisor: $58,902
8. Real estate broker: $58,720
9. Elevator installers and repairer: $58,710
10. Sales representative: $58,580
11. Dental hygienist: $58,350
12. Radiation therapist: $57,700
13. Nuclear medicine technologist: $56,450
14. Fraud investigator: $53,900
15. Criminal investigators special agent: $53,990
16. Immigration and customs inspector: $53,990
17. Police detective: $53,990
18. Police identification and records officer: $53,990
19. Commercial pilot: $53,870

Unemployed Graduates

For the first time in history, more people *with* degrees find themselves unemployed than people *without* degrees. As of May 2012, 52% of unemployed individuals were college graduates.[15] The trend has been headed this way for decades, as high school graduates have been able to land more jobs, and college graduates fewer jobs. As of July

2012, nearly two million college graduates with degrees are unemployed.[16] As one example of college graduates who struggle to find employment, in the year 2006 alone, 37,000 people graduated with a degree in history, but there were only 500 job openings available for them in that field.[17] History majors are not alone. There are fewer and fewer positions available for graduates who majored in amorphous topics such as area studies, anthropology, philosophy, and psychology.

Some think if they will continue on to graduate school that their chances of finding a job will be better. This is not necessarily true. The number of people with masters degrees and doctorates who are on welfare has tripled in three years (2007 to 2010)[18] as a result of unemployment among the overqualified.

One headline in *The Chronicle of Higher Education* pathetically stated, "Master's in English: Will Mow Lawns."[19] Some graduates do not seriously consider the career options that will or will not be open to them until after they graduate. Then, with creditors demanding loan payment, grads are desperate to find work in any field, not just that of their major. Often they find success in areas outside their major, yet are left with student loans to remind them of how they did not consider openings in the job market while in school. Talk to the neighbors up and down your street; you may be surprised how many of them are paying for degrees they do not need for their current careers.

Sixty-nine percent of jobs do not require a college degree, according to the Labor Department[20] and, according to the Bureau of Labor Statistics (BLS), "25 percent of college graduates are currently in jobs that do not require a college degree."[21] So, this means "17 million college-educated Americans are now working jobs for which they are overqualified. The BLS reports that hundreds of thousands of college graduates are working as waiters, secretaries, receptionists, laborers or janitors, all respectable occupations, but not jobs that will enable them to repay their five- or even six-digit college loans."[22] How much better it would be if they had obtained these jobs right away, and skipped taking on debt. They would have been so much further ahead financially. Better yet, without the pressure of having to repay loans, they likely would have been more entrepreneurial and able to earn money for work in which they were personally interested.

Is a degree worth all this financial drain? There has to be another way to success that does not involve such exorbitant cost. Many are waking up and proclaiming that the college experience is not valuable enough to merit a lifetime of financial stress. One of these "trumpet blowers," Dennis Prager, "urges college students and their parents to evaluate the value of going into debt for a college education in which students are bombarded for four years with withering criticism of every major value they hold."[23]

God's way of blessing has never involved debt (see Deuteronomy 28:12: "You shall lend to many nations, but you shall not borrow"), and debt is not necessary in order to eventually achieve success and sufficient income. As Proverbs states, "The blessing of the Lord makes one rich, and He adds no sorrow with it" (Proverbs 10:22).

No-Degree Testimony: Success in Architecture

"By following the Creator's ways, I now make a six-figure income without having a college degree. When I finished high school with a GPA lower than 2.0, I did not have many options available to me, nor did I wish to pursue further education at that particular point. I was not sure what I wanted to do with my life. Eventually, I began working in the IT field.

After a number of years and promotions, my employer encouraged me to further my education so I could be promoted to higher positions. So, I began to look at different colleges, and settled on Colorado Christian University because of the speed that I would be able to attain my degree and because they had a devotional period at the beginning of each class. After attending the mandatory classes on both evolution and world religions (which did not even include a Christian perspective), it was apparent to me that this Christian university was controlled by an authority other than the Word, and therefore could not provide a biblical form of education.

After a year of classes, I was convicted that I had been seeking man's education, knowing that the Creator promises provision, success and wealth by both man's standard and, more importantly, His standard (see Deuteronomy 8:10-20, 28:1-14; Psalm 1, 25:8-14; Matthew 6:25-34; and 3 John 2-4 for a few examples). I concluded that the type of higher education I was paying for was not one supported by the Creator, so I decided to not continue pursuing my degree.

Within several months of leaving school, I was promoted to lead engineer, the position that I was told I could not be promoted to without a college education! A year later, a larger company sought me and, without interviewing, offered me their lead architect position–offering greater benefits and a larger salary. Two years later, I was offered a senior solutions architect position with a Fortune 500 company. This was again without interviews or my own seeking. The Heavenly Father has placed me in a position where I am able to work from home and make more than a six-figure income.

I attribute all this to the promises of the Creator and allowing Him to fulfill those promises by seeking His ways above man's and seeking knowledge of Him. Abram and Sarai strove to fulfill the Heavenly Father's promises their own way, and it resulted in Hagar giving birth to Ishmael (Galatians 4:21-31). May we all allow Him to work in our lives and not seek to fulfill His promises through compromised means."

—BEAU BEAMSDERFER, husband, father of three, architect

5

Misplaced Missionaries

"You are the salt of the earth. But if the salt loses its saltiness, how can it be made salty again? It is no longer good for anything, except to be thrown out and trampled underfoot." (Matthew 5:13 NIV)

"I want to see at least one child in every class in every public school in America who is trained as a witness for Jesus Christ." This vision of Franklin Graham's is the mindset that many carry over to the college arena as well. They think, "We need Christians on campuses to be salt and light; otherwise universities will become wicked *really* fast, without the restraining and impacting influence of believers."

There is a major problem with the salt-and-light argument, and that is, students are not legally allowed to say "Jesus is Lord" in school anymore. Look at the graduation speeches valedictorians have tried to make, quoting

Scripture and thanking God for their success. They are often not allowed to do so. In some cases, the microphone is powered off right in the middle of their sentence.

It is not a feasible position to go to college as a "missionary." If a student really stands up for what she believes in class, she will not be able to remain there long. If she gets expelled, should she apply to another college and face getting expelled again? How many times would she be able to repeat the process?

How long would her grade remain passable when she stands for biblical creation rather than evolution on Biology tests? What about when she writes philosophy papers that boldly state that objective right and wrong exists? Or when she differs with her professor in a required religion class by explaining how it is impossible for every religion to be equally valid, because if they're all right, then they're all wrong?

Some will say that artfully questioning professors is a good way to expose errors in their teaching. However, this is not always received well. In her college days, my mother took a class under a professor who believed that people could be saved, but he did not believe in hell. When she gently questioned him as to what a person is saved from if hell does not exist, the professor became furious and refused to answer. She found out later that he was having an affair with one of the students in the class.

Try writing a position paper with a questioning stance, and see how good of a grade it gets. Chances are, even if the argument you present is logically solid, if it prods your professor in a vulnerable area, your grade will reflect his or her discomfort. In such a situation, your only options are either to hide your beliefs or to continue to be forthright and risk flunking.

Even if questioning professors somehow works for a while, there comes a point when a believer has to stand up for what she believes, and then questions are not sufficient.

Jen Keeton is one example of the impossibility of remaining in college if a student truly stands for her beliefs. A *World Net Daily* article entitled "Lose Christianity or Face Expulsion" tells the story of twenty-four-year-old Jen. As a master's degree candidate in counseling at Augusta State University, she stated that she personally believed that homosexuality was a behavioral choice, rather than a state of being. Though no one had any problem with her counseling ability, nor were there any complaints about her treatment of gay clients, the university decided that her Christian views were unacceptable.

Augusta State created a remediation plan that was required just for her, to alter her beliefs by immersing her into assigned homosexual literature and events. In response to this, she sued the university. Her lawsuit documents stated that school official "Anderson-Wiley confirmed that Miss Keeton will not be able to successfully complete the remediation plan and thus complete the (Augusta State University) counseling program unless she commits to affirming the propriety of gay and lesbian relationships if such an opportunity arises in her future professional efforts."[1] Senior Counsel David French of the Alliance Defending Freedom "contended [that] a public university student 'shouldn't be threatened with expulsion for being a

Christian and refusing to publicly renounce her faith, but that's exactly what's happening here.' "[2]

So it is evident that if we stand for everything we believe and consistently question teaching that is not consistent with Scripture, our college days will not last long. Jen Keeton was not even blatant with her beliefs—she was *asked* to state her position regarding homosexuality. The administration pulled it out of her, and then refused to allow her to graduate when she did not recant.

"Go for the Grade, But Hold to Your Own Opinion"

Some conclude that it is worth compromising to get a good grade and earn a diploma, even if that means writing assignments from positions that go against one's values. However, it is an unrealistic assumption to believe that one can write what the professor wants to hear but still hold to one's own private view on the subject. Four to eight years of that double standard, and a student is so torn up inside that she doesn't know what she believes. Worse, students often concede to the archenemy's viewpoint because they have become convinced from all the practice of arguing for that side while muzzling their own logic.

A person grows to believe in what she writes, talks, and is passionate about. Even if she initially disagrees with what she feels required to write and say, having another worldview constantly prevail is a dangerous fire to stoke. A subversive worldview may not stay on the surface of her thought life forever; it very well may end up supplanting her own worldview. This is what makes brainwashing successful.

After just two semesters of college, I found this happening to me. I would think a thought, and then, as I analyzed it, I would be shocked at the ideology I had bought into *unwillingly.* Feeling pressure to say the lingo in class, and being immersed in a world where the only valid ideologies were the ones presented by liberal professors, brought me to a place where my brain was beginning to think that way automatically, even outside of schoolwork. This was frightening to me!

For example, I have loved babies all my life and I pray for the day when the Lord may bless me with them as a mother, but I remember the moment at college when I was walking down my dorm hallway and thought, "Yes, it would make sense to put off marriage and having children until I have a successful career. A woman can impact more people through her career anyway. A family kind of wastes all that potential." On some subconscious level, I had identified with the feminist mindset. The real me, buried deep down inside, nearing extinction, stood up flabbergasted at this thought, but it had shriveled too small under the constant barrage of college life to be able to give an answer to that feminist plan of robbery.

It took me months after leaving college to get my head back on straight, and to once again embrace the realization that the impact a mother has on her children is far greater than any minuscule impact a career woman might have. As one woman in the professional world admitted:

"With all my customer contacts, employee supervision, and peer contact, my total influence doesn't constitute a drop in the bucket to what a wife and mother contributes to society. ... She has the power to make her home heaven or hell. That's what I call woman power."[3]

The Messiah Himself chose to pour His life into twelve people. They, not the masses, received most of His time and attention. The model of motherhood is the same.

It was a relief to me to rein my subconscious thinking back into line with my beliefs after they did the splits at college. I had not even taken a class on feminism—it was simply a prevailing undercurrent at the presupposition level on campus.

So, operating with a professor's ideology in order to get a good grade does not leave a student's faith unsinged. It is a perilous strategy.

Missionary Mindset Not Working

Even if there was a way for students to remain on campus without compromising their biblical convictions, the missionary mindset is not working. After just a few semesters, the statistics reveal that Christians are not pulling the rest of campus up out of the muck, but rather campus life pulls most Christians down until there is no identifiable difference between them and their worldly peers.

The Bible states, "Do not be deceived: 'Bad company corrupts good morals.' " (1 Corinthians 15:33 NASB). The general company that campus life predominately offers is foolish and wicked. Thus, the good morals of a choice few

Christian students quickly become ineffective when they are submersed day after day in such a faith-eroding environment. Proverbs warns, "He who walks with wise men will be wise, but the companion of fools will suffer harm" (Proverbs 13:20).

Unhelpful College Habit #4: Peers, Not Elders

College living promotes a habit of relating almost exclusively with peers. No real-world families with children and/or the elderly are present on campus. Consequently, it is easy for students to forget about lifetime priorities in a four-year bubble of unreality. The absence of wise elders in young people's lives is sadly felt as they aim more and more toward the lowest common denominator instead of growing through the prudent counsel of those who have gone before.

Even on Christian campuses, there is a lack of wise elders—older people designated by God to pass on their wisdom to youth. As Proverbs repeatedly indicates, one is spared much folly through consulting with their elders (parents, grandparents, and family friends). A few professors on campus may take the role of godly elders; however, where are they when nightlife ramps up? They do not live in the dorms. Their restraining influence is absent from any interactions that are not directly in front of them in the classrooms. At home, on the other hand, young ladies have the benefit of living alongside elders day and night—asking their counsel when tough decisions surface, and receiving guidance if they do not see dangers lurking ahead.

As Matthew 5:13 warns, "if the salt loses its saltiness, how can it be made salty again? It is no longer good for anything, except to be thrown out and trampled underfoot." When Christian students see the salt they have sprinkled around campus trampled underfoot, their faith often withers in response. Most realize that their acquaintances do not desire their Christian "saltiness" anymore, so they conform and instead behave in whatever way *will* bring them acceptance. The college environment wears on even strong believers, until it becomes tempting for many (if not most) to give up being "salty."

Blessed is the Young Woman...

It is very revealing to apply Psalm 1 to the university setting in order to discover what God thinks of participating in college. Think about a typical college student as you read it, and consider whether or not she is the one this passage refers to as blessed:

> Blessed is the man who does not walk in the counsel of the wicked, or stand in the way of sinners, or sit in the seat of mockers. (Psalm 1:1 NIV)

Are you surprised at how opposite this is to the life of college students? College offers the *counsel of wicked* professors, who earnestly desire students to adhere to their liberal teaching; the unavoidable necessity of *standing in the way* of immoral acquaintances—*sinners* really; and finding oneself *sitting in the seat of mockers*, constantly having to hear the speech of those who do not fear their Creator. Notice the progression from walking, to standing around, to sitting down and becoming one of the group. What comes next? Lying down in the beds of the un-righteous?

This passage implies that the person who *does* walk in the counsel of the wicked, stand in the way of sinners, and sit in the seat of mockers will receive the opposite of blessing. If Psalm 1 is true, is it even possible to be blessed as a college student? The author is not even going so far as to say that a person will be cursed if he *becomes* wicked; he will not be blessed if he simply *associates* with those who are. (A godly young lady may be able to find a few Christian friends at college, but she still has to relate with other, not so wholesome, students on a daily basis.)

As the sages say, "Show me a man's friends today and I will show you who he will be tomorrow." Do we desire to become like the majority of godless college students? Proverbs encourages us, "Do not be envious of evil men, nor desire to be with them" (Proverbs 24:1).

Do we desire to be like the righteous man of Psalm 1, instead? The way to imitate him is by *not* walking in the counsel, standing in the way, or sitting in the seat of those who do not fear God. Granted, it is *harder* to separate ourselves from participating in these three patterns than to go with the flow, but the direct connection with God that results from obedience makes leaving worth it.

Once we have decided to choose to be separate from the companionship of the ungodly, we can echo young Jeremiah, who prayed:

> Know that for Your sake I have suffered rebuke. ... Your Word was to me the joy and rejoicing of my heart; for I am called by Your name, O Lord God of hosts. I did not sit in the assembly of the mockers, nor did I rejoice; I sat alone because of Your hand, for You have filled me with indignation. (Jeremiah 15:15-17)

It's okay to "keep oneself from being polluted by the world." In fact, doing so is "the religion that God our Father accepts as pure and faultless," according to James 1:27. Do you want to be blessed? The path to blessing is plainly laid out in Psalm 1.

Engaging Culture

Some people contend that choosing a path other than college equates to retreating from the scene of battle. They contend that we must stay in college to be able to influence the culture.

Yes, it is important to interact with the culture, and uplift it for our King, but it is far better to reach out from our own free-speech turf, rather than a from a restricted college campus. Hospitality is a prime way to impact people. Inviting other families into one's home for them to experience the full warmth of a Christian lifestyle has the potential for far more influence than trying to have a debate for the truth in a censored classroom under a professor who is bent on promoting his or her own agenda. In a classroom, the professor decides what will and will not be acceptable, while in one's own home, one can feel free to share deeply. The person in charge of the playing field gets to set the game rules.

When students need to seek approval from their college in order to graduate, the extent to which they can impact and change their college culture lessens. To achieve top grades, it is necessary to have exposure to immoral content (in order to discuss it knowledgably in class) and to write from godless perspectives. A's are not given to students who challenge what they are taught in order to impact thought in the classroom. As we have seen, world changers for the Messiah are not welcomed in their classes if they stand for truth.

Culture changing does not happen effectively by integrating with the culture. Think of a righteous man who feels called to witness in a bar, and take note of his strategy. He goes in there, "engages the culture" with the gospel, and then gets out as soon as his mission is accomplished. Hanging out in the place of temptation will not accomplish any more good; in fact, doing so has been proven to cause weaker "missionaries" to become desensitized to evil and worn down by constant pressure to join the crowd. We can be more effective by not being immersed in college life than by identifying with the very culture we are called to impact.

6

CHUCKING COLLEGE

" 'Behold, the fear of the Lord, that is wisdom, and to depart from evil is understanding.' "
(Job 28:28)

What will it profit a girl if she gains the whole world but loses her soul, her lifetime financial freedom, her purity, her love of reading, her unique individuality, her entrepreneurial momentum, and four peak years of her life? A college degree may no longer be worth the world to us when we see what we have to surrender for it. The costs for that piece of paper—financial, emotional, spiritual, and temporal—rise higher with every graduation.

"For what will it profit a man if he gains the whole world, and loses his own soul?" (Mark 8:36) was one of the verses that helped me decide it was time to leave college. As a cellist, I had the opportunity of traveling to

Vienna with the college symphony orchestra and playing in the world-famous concert hall where the Vienna Philharmonic televises their annual New Year's Eve concert. But I realized that most of the students would drink heavily in Europe, where the legal drinking age is lower. In fact, I could not even find two acquaintances who would agree with me not to drink on the trip in order to visit historic sites instead. By going on the tour, I would have been under constant peer pressure while immorality ran fast and loose at night in the hotels.

So there I was that April—my freshman year coming to an end. I knew my choices: gaining "the whole world" and losing my soul (which the whole college environment was wearing down), or chucking college and finding a path of success where my faith could thrive. The faith-eroding atmosphere at college was too calculated for me to hope to keep both Vienna and my soul. (Imagining now what would remain of my faith if I had endured another year or two or *three!* of college frightens me. I know that I would have been on shaky ground at best. But, praise the King, He had other plans for me.) I gradually realized the seriousness of my remaining in college, and began my exodus.

Doug Phillips has said, "College is a trip through Babylon. If the academics don't get you, the dorm life will." The Creator's forbearance toward all the immorality rampant in dorm life and the misinterpretation of His Word prevalent in classrooms will eventually come to an end. He is a righteous Judge, and like He did with Sodom, He will judge those who are immersed in a culture of lawlessness. So, when Scripture states, "Come out of her, my people, lest you share in her sins, and lest you receive of her plagues" (Revelation 18:4), let us not be like Lot and his daughters who had to be dragged out at the last minute by the angels.

Proverbs 16:17 declares, "The highway of the upright is to depart from evil; he who keeps his way preserves his soul." Righteous people depart from evil environments and evil teachings. According to Scripture, the descriptive characteristic of the righteous is that they are set-apart and holy—not loitering and trying to survive in the midst of those who habitually practice sin.

> "I guide you in the way of wisdom and lead you along straight paths. ... Do not set foot on the path of the wicked or walk in the way of evil men. Avoid it, do not travel on it; turn from it and go on your way ... and take only ways that are firm."
> (Proverbs 4:11, 14-15, 26 NIV)

The Question of Needing a Degree

When we really think it over, a degree may not be necessary to equip us for each of our life purposes. Many college graduates discover (after the fact) that a degree was not a prerequisite for their success.

For example, one twenty-two-year-old young man majored in finance, but then went on to start his own business selling precious metals. His real-life experience was more helpful to him than his actual degree, and, of course, in running his own business, he did not need to have that degree in order to become highly successful.

In another example, a musically inclined young lady realized that she would not need a music degree in order to be a successful professional musician. Skilled musicians can teach lessons and make $20-$30 an hour, with no one concerned about whether they have a degree or not. Skill is what is most sought-after—a well-performed audition will land a musician a job in a symphony orchestra, while a degree in music performance alone will not guarantee the position.

Or, for the would-be English major, a well-written essay with a resume listing all the instances where her works have been published carries more weight in a job application than a college degree with no work experience accompanying it.

In the great majority of cases, possessing skills can carry one farther than having earned a degree. Proverbs 22:29 does not mention the need for a university degree, but rather states, "Do you see a man skilled in his work? He will stand before kings; He will not stand before obscure men."

Therefore, we need to think hard and think creatively to analyze if there is some way to fulfill our callings without dragging ourselves through Sodom simply for a costly piece of paper that declares, "You did it!" In his article, "For Most People, College is a Waste of Time," Charles Murray discusses the arbitrary and questionable value of college degrees:

First, we set up a single goal to represent educational success, which will take four years to achieve, no matter what is being taught. We attach an economic reward to it that seldom has anything to do with what has been learned. We urge large numbers of people who do not possess adequate ability to try to achieve the goal, wait until they have spent a lot of time and money, and then deny it to them. We ... stigmatize everyone who doesn't meet the goal. We ... call the goal a "B.A." ... Outside a handful of majors—engineering and some of the sciences—a bachelor's degree tells an employer nothing except that the applicant has a certain amount of intellectual ability and perseverance. Even a degree in a vocational major like business administration can mean anything from a solid base of knowledge to four years of barely remembered gut courses.

The solution is not better degrees, but no degrees. ... The model is the CPA exam that qualifies certified public accountants. [It is standardized across the nation, rigorous, and shows how much the person really knows about accounting.] ... Why not present [students] with certifications in microbiology or economics [instead of diplomas]—and who cares if the applicants passed the exam after studying in the local public library. ... Under a certification system, four years is not required, residence is not required, expensive tuitions are not required, and a degree is not required. Equal educational opportunity means, among other things, creating a society in which it's what you know that makes the difference. Substituting certifications for degrees would be a big step in that direction ...

Certification tests would disadvantage just one set of people: students who have gotten into well-known traditional schools, but who are coasting through their years in college and would score poorly on a certification test. Disadvantaging them is an outcome devoutly to be wished. ...

The demonstration of competency in business administration or European history would, appropriately, take on similarities to the demonstration of competency in cooking or welding. Our obsession with the BA has created a two-tiered entry to adulthood, anointing some for admission to the club and labeling the rest as second-best. ... Getting rid of the BA and replacing it with evidence of competence [would eliminate that stigma].[1]

Europe already employs this system of certificates for job-specific training such as apprenticeships. However, before the United States realizes what an improvement certifications would be over degrees, we can individually seek similar alternative routes of advanced education that result in competence rather than necessarily a diploma.

Colin Campbell (husband of Nancy Campbell, the founder of *Above Rubies*) shared with me his perspective regarding biblical alternatives to college. He mentioned that as a shepherd boy, David did not study harp under a humanist professor. He practiced and practiced out in the sheep pasture under the inspiration of the Holy Spirit. His diligent autonomous practice on the harp brought his skill to such a level that it prepared a place for him in the king's palace. Likewise, turning from college does not imply that we are to also give up on advanced education or perfecting our talents. Skills are vitally important to bring glory to the Name of God. Excellence is a work's glory. So we must look for unique ways to develop our skills without necessarily conforming to the college cookie-cutter pattern. Training and education do exist outside the liberal college package.

As daughters at home, this often means switching our priorities from one specific goal (such as majoring in English, Biology, or music), to becoming capable in many areas, like a skilled First Lady in the White House. Jackie Kennedy was an exemplary First Lady. She was known for her strong communication skills and social graces. She worked at restoring the interior of the White House, and decorating it with skill. She is remembered for her excellent organizational skills, and she is said to have personally tasted meals before important dignitaries arrived— instructing the cooks on how to improve the flavor of a dish. As one news article stated, "Jackie elevated presidential entertaining into occasions imbued with culture. She personally choreographed every detail of state dinners so they would project the Kennedy image of vitality and sophistication."[2] She was intelligent, and loved history, which was advantageous in her conversations with dignitaries.

This is the type of all-around excellence to which we should aim as daughters at home. It should be our goal to become confident and well-versed in hospitality, sewing, and cooking, to be knowledgeable about alternative health, well-read in history and biographies, and, in addition, to pursue individual areas of academic prowess in any free time. Being at home should appear no narrower to us than it did to First Lady Jackie Kennedy in the White House.

Having to spend all one's time jumping through an institution's contemporarily-hip course hoops makes it very difficult to find the time to master domestic skills we will need as first ladies in our future homes. If a young woman spends four to eight years debating worldly philosophy and studying for a career, she is simply not going to possess as much competence in running a home and living a life of self-sacrifice for her man and her babies as the young woman who has been practicing those skills daily. College saps valuable time from preparing for the life many of us hope to live someday—that of a wife and mother.

Economists use the term "opportunity cost" to describe this type of loss. They underscore the importance of evaluating opportunity cost when making a decision. Simply put, if a person spends money or time on one thing, he or she cannot spend the same on another thing. Opportunity cost is the cost of not being able to do something else with that time or money. We need to consider the opportunity cost of spending the four peak preparation years of our lives in college. If we truly aspire to be homemakers one day, the opportunity cost of not being able to invest time and preparation into skills we will need daily may be more than we want to sacrifice.

Being a stay-at-home daughter in the twenty-first century brings with it a weight of pioneering, even though there have been only a few recent generations in which daughters sought careers. Before that, the norm for most of history involved daughters being productive from their home base. Breaking away from our culture's current expectations and returning to the biblical model is a challenge, though it can bring great fulfillment.

Successful role models are beacons of the joy of stay-at-home daughterhood. Two such examples come from the lives of the Botkin sisters, authors of two excellent books: *So Much More,* and *It's Not (That) Complicated.* Their bio at visionarydaughters.com includes the remark that "they delight in discovering … and in investigating the glorious and diverse opportunities open to young women at home." May that increasingly become our delight as well.

What Will People Think?

One of the primary reasons it is so hard to take any route other than college after high school is the fear of what people will think. Ego. Peer pressure.

> "Education may be the only thing people still believe in in the United States. To question education is really dangerous. It is the absolute taboo. It's like telling the world there's no Santa Claus."
>
> —PETER THIEL, cofounder of PayPal and founder of the *20 Under 20 Thiel Fellowship*

As one author pointed out, "If Harvard were only about learning, very few people would be willing to pay a quarter of a million dollars [to go there]. The knowledge and training certainly could be obtained for a fraction of that cost."[3] So it is not just the promise of an education that attracts us to college. We are concerned that relatives and acquaintances will think of us as failures if we do not obtain a four-year degree.

Our culture treats the college decision as if it is the most serious choice of a person's entire life. People give it such overwhelming importance that the subliminal message is that youth will self-destruct if they do not go.

So, should we tremble under the withering presence of controlling "college or fail" comments? The Bible says, "The fear of man brings a snare" (Proverbs 29:25 NASB), and experience proves the truth of that. Often other people's opinions sway us from doing what we would do if no one else had any influence on our decisions. Perhaps it would strengthen our resolve to thoroughly realize that on Judgment Day each of us will stand alone before our Maker, having to answer for our decisions without others there to evaluate what we have done based on what *they* would prefer. No matter what we decide to do with our lives, someone will always disagree. We become snared when we doubt what we should do in response to people's negative comments about our choices. Job spoke about this universal tendency when he echoed the reasons people often give for doing other than right, "because I so feared the crowd, and the contempt of families terrified me," (Job 31:34 NIV, NASB).

That those who pressure us young people to go to college will later exert pressure about getting married (by probing questions like, "How are your relationships with young men these days?" Or, "Better find somebody soon!"). Then, later in life, they might apply pressure about having children (either about taking "too long" to have children, or about having "too many"). Remembering that pressure from people will extend further than our college choices is freeing when we decide to unhook from their expectations. People come from completely different worldview perspectives on every issue. College is just *one* of those issues.

As speaker S. M. Davis encourages, "Don't allow it to bother you when a sick world laughs at you for having enough sense to stay morally and spiritually healthy by not drinking out of their contaminated well."[4] If we choose to leave the college system because of how little it honors God, *we* actually stand on solid ground, not those who continue on at college. We can turn the tables when threatened about our choice to not go, and thoughtfully ask continuing students whether they are sure *they* are doing the right thing in remaining.

Moses promised the judges of the people of Israel, "you shall not be afraid in any man's presence" (Deuteronomy 1:17). This is possible because, in Solomon's words, "the righteous are bold as a lion" (Proverbs 28:1). Great peace comes from the life example of the Son of God, for Whom (as the missionary Geoffrey Bull writes) "the company of the Father outweighed all the ostracism of the world. ... He had nothing else to be or do on earth beyond the requirements of the Father."[5]

Of course, it is right to heed wise advice that is in agreement with biblical principles. However, when people stir up doubt and fear through their opinions rather than sharing direction from Scripture, we might as well do what we feel *God* calling us to do, without concerning ourselves too much about what others think. The end of the verse, "The fear of man brings a snare" is, "but he who trusts in the Lord will be exalted" (Proverbs 29:25). If we fear what the Creator thinks of our decision more than what people think, we will experience His blessing. A Vietnamese Christian pastor who was imprisoned for his faith once said, "We have learned that suffering is not the worst thing in the world—disobedience to God is the worst."[6] And the same with the wee bit of suffering that might come our way for choosing to obey the Creator by departing from evil at college. Being ridiculed is not the worst thing in the world, disobedience is.

We need not long for the praise of the world if we are believers. Our Master's praise is of far greater worth. Geoffrey Bull eloquently relegated the world's praise with these words:

> The world's esteem and assessment of human brilliance and achievement, the total of human activity viewed in its alienation from the living God, has absolutely no food for the new man, and its approbation [approval and praise] is worthless.[7]
>
> Let us not be afraid of remaining unexplained ... Enoch was unaccounted for. He had gone on with God.[8]

Prepare for Attack

If you choose to chuck college, expect attacks from the enemy through friends and family and even personal doubts. Choosing to abandon the world's expectations for higher education is not emotionally easy. The way to be ready is to be armed. Sharpen your spiritual sword by immersion in Scripture and by practicing responses through role-playing possible conversations. For instance, instead of saying in a glum voice, "Yeah, I'm not going to college ... I'm just going to hang out around home," plan to respond with something like this: "I decided I don't have time to waste on a college administration's arbitrary requirements. I have a business I'm launching, and I'm busy from sun-up to sun-down studying exciting books on my own!" Think strategically in order to anticipate what confrontational angles people might take. Practice how to respond brightly and confidently to comments and doubts, so as not to be taken by surprise when various remarks strike.

Through each attack the Messiah asks us, "Do you love Me more than these?" (John 21:15). Do we love Him enough to not sacrifice our spiritual and moral vitality for a degree? Do we love Him more than friends' approval? Do we love Him more than our ego?

It takes strong resolve to choose to be successful in a different way than the majority of young people. A book written in 1852, *Letters to a Young Christian*, exhorts:

> You think you could go to a martyr's stake ... but there are some things in life which require more courage than that; one is, to dare to be singular; and another is, to make thorough work in the matter of crucifying self. [9]

The enemy does not want us to leave any area of his influence, so if we are "in the know" about his devastating college plans for youth, and we intend to avoid them, he will send attack en force to try to get us to minds. Be prepared.

> "It is the policy of the Tempter to send his solicitations by the hand of those whom we love, whom we least suspect of any ill design upon us, and whom we are desirous to please and apt to conform ourselves to. ... Satan tempted Adam by Eve and Christ by Peter. We [should] therefore ... stand upon our guard against a bad proposal [even] when the person that makes it can pretend to an interest in us, that we many never sin against God in compliment to the best friend we have in the world."
> —MATTHEW HENRY, commentary on Deuteronomy 13:6

Longing for College

One method the enemy can use to try to lure us back under his spiritual tsunami, moral maelstrom, academic assault, and financial freefall, is to cause us to long for college. *He likes to make us feel like we are missing out, even when we are right in the center of the Lord's will.* Sure, it is easier to go to college than to be successful from home. College students are spoon-fed their assignments, while independent learners have to uniquely chart their own courses to success.

Yet, we should strengthen ourselves to not weep over the things of Egypt like the children of Israel did in Numbers 11:5-6. They said:

> "We remember the fish which we ate freely in Egypt, the cucumbers, the melons, the leeks, the onions, and the garlic; but now our whole being is dried up; there is nothing at all except this manna before our eyes!"

A few verses later in this passage Moses states that in response to their longing, "the anger of the Lord was greatly aroused." When He gives us unique avenues to success—such as manna in this case—we must restrain ourselves from longing for the treasures of Egypt instead of the gifts from His hand.

Satan desperately wants to remove young ladies from the protection of their fathers' homes. That could explain part of why young women sometimes think that they could be more productive anywhere else, other than at home. The enemy wants to destroy us, and cannot access us as easily while we remain under authority. Realizing this can help us feel validated at home, and release us to move on to be productive from the hub of our homes.

We can take encouragement from the historical fact that the Saviour Himself stayed home, subjected to His earthly authority, until He was thirty years old. He neither moved out on His own, nor sought higher education in Rome (the equivalent of college, perhaps). "He did not flourish personal credentials proclaiming personal achievements,"[10] yet the crowds said of His educated deportment, "How does this Man know letters, having never studied?" (John 7:15).

He had to deal with family dynamics (imagine the sibling rivalry among His four brothers and at least two sisters*) and carry the responsibility of their home business (since, according to tradition, Joseph—His earthly father—passed away when He was about nineteen years old). He felt His call all through those eighteen silent years of faithfulness at home (from age twelve in the temple to age thirty when His public ministry began). It burned within Him, yet He was not released to fulfill it. When the Heavenly Father said, "This is My son in whom I am well pleased," the Messiah had not done anything miraculous yet. But He had been obedient as a Son at home, subjecting Himself to parental authority.[11] We think it stretches *us* to be at home, single, when we're in our twenties? The Author and Perfector of our faith—God Himself—did it!

As Psalm 84:10 declares, "For a day in Your courts is better than a thousand. I would rather be a doorkeeper in the house of my God than dwell in the tents of wickedness." A house is permanent, while a tent is transitory, thus a servant position in a house is of greater value than a position of honor in a tent. If we consider dorms to be brewing places of wickedness, then we can easily admit that one day in the King's service is worth a thousand days enduring wickedness in college—the "tents of the wrong."

A few days before the devoted Christian singer Keith Green went home to be with the Lord, he had a fresh burden on his heart that he wrote about in an article

---

* James, Joseph, Judas, Simon, and sisters (Matthew 13:55-56).

entitled "Why YOU Should Go to The Mission Field." In the article, he wrote a bold statement about college. As an answer to the objection, "But I need to get an education first!" he wrote, "You shouldn't go to college unless God has definitely called you to go."[12] This man was sold out for the King throughout his entire music ministry. The closeness with which he walked with the Lord during his seven years of being a Christian (before he died at the age of twenty-eight) is representative of how he only had time for what the Father wanted him to do. There are Christians who do what everyone else does, and there are Christians who want to walk as close to God's highest plan for them as possible. Keith Green's statement about college is a statement by a man from the latter category. Do we long to go to college because everyone else is going, or do we long first and foremost to do what God has called us to do?

This proverb from the wisest man who ever lived can help us to be firm: "Do not let your heart envy sinners, but be zealous for the fear of the Lord all the day; for surely there is a hereafter, and your hope will not be cut off" (Proverbs 23: 17-18).

Remember Lot's Wife!

Our decisions have no less impact than Lot's wife's. We may think we are the only people they affect, but the body of Christ is watching and hangs on us to choose rightly. Will we women face home life that may appear to be a limited "cave" with joy and purpose, or will we long for the transient fulfillment offered us by colleges and careers of Sodom?

Often the Heavenly Father does great things through people who find themselves in cave-like places as a result of obedience to his will. Consider Daniel in a den of lions, when it seemed to be the end of his life; Elijah in a cave, feeling like he was the only believer left; David hiding in caves from a king who wanted to take his life; and the Messiah, when it appeared that He had failed, because He died and was buried in a cave. The chronicle of faith in Hebrews 11 declares, "the world was not worthy of them. They wandered in deserts and mountains, and in caves and holes in the ground."[13]

It is okay, according to the sovereign Creator, that our lives have times of journeying through barren places, steep mountains of trial, or dark caves that seem at first to have no outlet for creative expression or impact on the world. For, it is in the desert that we most cry out to God for His Son, the living water, and it is in that cave that we, like Elijah, are privileged to hear that still small voice of the Father (see 1 Kings 19). The dark place does not last forever. There is glory after trial, as 1 Peter 5:10 encourages, "But may the God of all grace, who called us to His eternal glory by Christ Jesus, after you have suffered a while, perfect, establish, strengthen, and settle you."

Many fame-bringing actions that the world extols are essentially the same as faithful deeds that are done unnoticed at home. The only difference is that the former are performed in the limelight. Which will receive the greater reward in eternity, however? Without a doubt, the silent, selfless faithfulnesses will. In contrast, what becomes of the coveted self-indulgent fame? It is limited to earth. Matthew 6:2-4 states about those who receive the world's praise, "Truly I say to you, they have received their reward in full..." but it goes on to say about those whose acts go unseen, "Then your Father, Who sees what is done in secret will reward you." There 'tis. Perhaps the world will be impacted by our lives; perhaps not. Our sole motivation should not be desiring its acclaim, but rather being faithful in what we are called to do.

What Next?

In "The College Illusion" issue of *Whistleblower* magazine, David Kupelian wrote in his editorial:

> The idea, unquestioned for generations, that college is the ideal destination for all high-schoolers—the notion that even those who have no particular interests or career focus should just go to college anyway, take courses, meet people, enjoy the wild social life, and try to obtain some sort of four-year degree while racking up crushing debt—is increasingly being questioned ... and rejected. ... All that is necessary is to break free of the paralyzing fear that not graduating from college will result in failure. It's not true.[14]

The individuals who have been successful throughout history without a degree confirm the truth that not graduating from college does *not* automatically result in failure. See Appendix B to read the impressive "College Dropouts Hall of Fame"—a list of people who have proved this.

The eminent theologian Dietrich Bonhoeffer (known for his opposition efforts in Nazi Germany) made the statement, "If you board the wrong train it is no use running along the corridor in the opposite direction." So what is the right "train" to board? If we believe that home is the God-ordained place for young women to continue to grow after their formal education is completed, then how do we most effectively redeem the time at home?

Frances Havergal, who wrote the hymn "Take My Life and Let It Be" once shared, "Every 'kept *from,*' should have its corresponding and still more blessed 'kept *for.*' We do not want our moments to be simply kept from Satan's use, but kept for His use; we want them to be not only kept from sin, but kept for his praise."[15] The rest of this book will discuss ways to be highly successful without enduring the corrupting influences of most campuses.

Chucking College Testimony: Torn in Two

" My college experience spanned a period of seven years, three colleges, two majors, and thousands of dollars. At the end of it all I cannot even boast a bachelor's degree. My first major was in fashion design, but shortly after getting my associate's degree in that, I realized the fashion industry was not for me. My parents wanted me to go to college for a career with stability and income. I had an interest in midwifery, but that career didn't fit either of those requirements, so I decided to begin the process of entering the nursing program at our local community college.

While I was part way through my prerequisites for nursing school, I took my first trip to Israel. That was a major mile-marker in my life. I felt that was where God was calling me to serve. I also started receiving the *Above Rubies* magazine and saw an article in the August 2006 issue about the Waller family. Their family ministry—HaYovel—serves the vineyard owners in Israel by pruning and harvesting with them, so I was immediately drawn to their love for the land of Israel. I then watched a documentary about them called *A Journey Home.* I saw purity and peace in their life, instead of the confusion I had faced in college. As a result of their inspiration, I began making some drastic changes in my life and decided nursing wasn't my end goal—I wanted to be a wife and mother.

I looked into quitting school for good at that point but my parents didn't see how that was going to work. My life had centered around school and preparing for a career for so long that I felt a lack of direction and motivation at home. I was getting older and so was my father. Without a prospect of marriage at hand, my parents wanted me to be able to support myself, so I returned to college to honor them.

My life seemed like an oxymoron. I felt the Father calling me to Israel and to be a wife and mother. A nursing career didn't seem to prepare me for either. Everything around me in college was pushing me down, and I had to fight hard to keep climbing back up, step-by-step. My dilemma became even more exaggerated after we met the Wallers personally and they invited me to come to the harvest in Israel with them. I tried everything I could think of to be able to go, but I cried many tears when I finally succumbed to the fact that I had to stay home with school and work.

I also didn't know how the husband I longed for was going to find me in the middle of this situation. My concerns were enforced as I watched the movie *The Return of the Daughters*. A line from one of the young men in the video kept running over and over in my head. He said, "I wasn't looking for a woman who was going to nursing school—I was looking for someone who would be capable in the home."

While I was still going to school, the Wallers stayed with us for a week before going to Israel. After they left our house, Mr. and Mrs. Waller told their oldest son, Brayden, that they thought I might be the one to be his wife. This was a very unexpected turn of events because of how completely different we both are. I was known for my artsy flair and he was known for his simplicity.

During their next visit after returning from Israel, Brayden had a dream, confirming to him that I was to be his wife. I still did not know anything about that possibility. I was a mess at that time, because someone else was interested in me, so I sought counsel from Mrs. Waller. She was very firm in advising me to "Just wait," and said she was sure God had a better plan in store for me. Little did I know!

A week later, Brayden called my dad. It was a week of battle for me. I had college projects and papers due, and I also dreaded having to tell Brayden about things in my past. Brayden was the one by whom I always measured every other young man, because of his ardent love of the Lord. But I never imagined he would want to marry me! The enemy tried to tell me I was worthless because of the mistakes I had made while in college and public high school, and I wondered if I should cut off any possibility of a relationship for his sake. When I finally told him about my past, his forgiveness was great, and he said that he wanted to look past my compromises and love me the way the Savior does.

As we pursued betrothal, I was still studying at college, telling Brayden that I felt like I got slimed every time I went to school. So Brayden shared with my dad that he didn't feel like I would need to have a degree after we got married, and that he didn't feel comfortable becoming my spiritual head while I was still in college. If I was going to stay in school, Brayden said we'd have to delay the betrothal. So, my parents agreed to let me quit one semester before I was to get my degree, which was such a relief to me! Not long after, we got betrothed, and then married.

I feel like The Heavenly Father, in His perfect plan, has used some of my college education for good, but the price was high. I would never want to pay it again and I wouldn't send my children to pay the price either.

Do you need college to be successful? How do you define success? The world will give you its standard but often it is far from the standard that God sets. In most cases, college will teach you to think, work, and make decisions that promote *yourself* and will help you to advance to the next step in *your* plan (or their plan for you). The Father's plan is for us to promote *Him* and see *His* plan go forward on this earth.

His plan has given my life vision and excitement. I have served in Israel for fifteen months out of my three-and-a-half years (so far) of married life, and ministry is leading us to parts of the world that I never thought I would visit. The zeal I used to have for my own plan has been turned to an even greater zeal for His plan.

The world will teach us to *take* when the Father wants us to lay it all down. I am still learning, but I know the more I lay down, the more I have seen the Father's hand in my life. Seek to discover His heart, to see Him glorified, and to see His plan go forth, and then you will find true fulfillment and true success."

—TALI WALLER, devoted wife and mother of two.
Featured in the documentary *Betrothed*
(Third Dawn LLC: 2010)

7

VOCATIONAL VISION

"Your ears shall hear a word behind you, saying,
'This is the way, walk in it.' "
(Isaiah 30:21)

So, what are we to do? It is evident that colleges breed immorality, strip away Bible-based beliefs, rarely provide a worthwhile education, and drain bank accounts as exorbitant tuition costs plunge students into debt. But how do we prepare for a lifelong vocation without college? Is it even possible?

To find vocational direction, first it is necessary to identify what we were each individually created to do. According (in part) to Webster's 1828 dictionary, the word "vocation" means: a calling by the will of God to a noble occupation, accompanied by a strong feeling of suitability for that particular work.

The question: "What do you want to be when you grow up?" is too open-ended to be of much help to most young people. However, three God-given parameters of one's existence make it much less vague to ascertain one's life purpose. To find one's niche in life, it is necessary to realize that one is first a Christian, then a woman, and finally an individual with specific talents.

Most career guidance only takes into account a young person's talents, but that actually is the final thing to consider, not the first. If the first two factors are ignored when seeking one's life vocation, a young lady might find herself working in a field where her talent can shine, but where her faith cannot thrive, or holding an office of authority that perhaps a woman ought not to have. As a result, she might find herself catapulted into unnecessary lifestyle stresses.

Therefore, we must look at the whole equation (not just talent) to determine what vocation God has called each of us to. As we look at each of these three areas, we can analyze what kind of education would best fit these para-meters as well.

As a Christian

In order to fully obey the Creator's commands, a Bible believer's often has to sacrifice something. This is true when choosing a vocation as well; being a Christian means there are some fields of work that we must not consider. No matter how skilled an individual is, if applying those skills in a certain arena means disobedience to the commands of Scripture, then doing so is not an option. For example, no matter how capable a young woman might be as a doctor's aide, serving an abortion doctor with that talent can never help her fulfill her God-given life mission, because it does not pass the first test of who she is: a Christian. A Christian has a heart to obey the sixth commandment: "Thou shall not murder."

Additional cases where career options do not pass this first guideline might include jobs that require deceit, immodest dress, working on the Sabbath, or breaking other biblical convictions. No temporal opportunity on this earth is worth jeopardizing eternal rewards as a result of compromising one's obedience to God's Word.

The story of Amaziah, king of Judah, offers a biblical example of turning from material gain to honor God's commands. Amaziah was about to go to war, so he hired 100,000 mighty men to join his army. But then a prophet of Yahweh came to stop Amaziah, and declared to him that it was not God's will for the hired men to go into battle with him. Amaziah was concerned, because he had already paid all the soldiers one hundred talents of silver. He would have taken quite a financial loss by letting the mercenaries go; however, the prophet said to him, " 'The Lord is able to give you much more than this' " (2 Chronicles 25:9). So, he believed that promise, and let the men go.

We too can remember the great encouragement of this verse whenever we sacrifice to obey the Word of God. Costly obedience is always worth it, if it is the price for maintaining a clear conscience before God. The Lord has more to give us than we have to sacrifice for Him.

out and submit to men who are not their God-given authorities as helpmates to them in the workforce.

When a woman tries to please one man at work and another man at home, her affections become divided, and her feminine beauty becomes hardened. Helen Andelin, in her book, *Fascinating Womanhood*, poetically reveals what a wife relinquishes if she works outside her home: "The moon, when it moves from its sphere of night into day, loses its luster, its charm, its very poetry."[1] When a woman's employments, delights, and ministries are based from her home, she radiates God's glory as no one else could in her stead. But when a woman invests her energy in a career outside of her home, she loses her feminine luster. In addition, she takes on a double curse—the man's curse in addition to the woman's (see Genesis 3:16-19). Andelin continues, "devotion to your household, family, and charity *enhances feminine charm,* whereas employment outside the home does little or nothing for it."[2] So, apart from the implication of divided loyalty with two different authorities, even the *practical* fruit of a woman choosing a career outside her home fails to equal the satisfying glory of homemaking.

If you desire to work because you find yourself bored at home, Andelin states, "the problem is that you are buying happiness at the expense of your family. You are putting your desires ahead of their needs. This is never justified."[3] She goes on to say, "Your child ... doesn't want you to be bright, talented, chic, or smart. ... He just wants you to love him. He will be the one who pays the price for your wanting to have it all."[4] So it is evident that not only does working for another man put a woman in relational compromise, but a career outside the home also does not allow a woman or her family to fully thrive— contrary to what feminists claim.

Women Are Irreplaceable

Women were created with special nurturing ability, with finesse to transform a house into a cozy home, with the opportunity to bear children, with tenderness in conversation with others, with the responsibility to creatively and faithfully provide nutritious and delicious food for their households, and with other unique capabilities. As Andelin writes:

> To be a successful mother is greater than to be a successful opera singer, writer, or artist. One is eternal greatness and the other a short-term honor. ... The work in the home is a different kind of glory than career woman enjoy. A great mother lives in obscurity, and the perfect wife is even less known. Her reward is a quiet unacclaimed honor. Her glory is the esteem of her husband, the happiness of her children, and her overall success in the home."[5]

Andelin also profoundly states, "Feminists fail to realize that someone must do the woman's work,"[6] and women do it best. Swapping roles will never be as fulfilling as doing the work for which we were designed.

Education As a Woman

As women, we were not created to be primary income-earners at any time in our lives. In the "what if" scenarios designed to show the necessity of obtaining a career-bringing degree: "What if Mr. Right never comes along and you are single forever?" or: "What if you are widowed and have children to provide for?", the biblical response in each case is that the woman is always protected under authority. In Bible days, if a maiden did not get married, she remained in her father's house and found a way to be economically productive from that home base. If she became widowed, she returned to her father's house (as Leviticus 22:13 assumes) or the church cared for her as a widow.

So, even in all of these what-if cases, the optimal way to obtain income as a woman comes from having skill to make money from home. This is how women in the Bible earned revenue—the Proverbs 31 woman, Lydia (a seller of purple cloth), and others. Titus 2:5 describes godly younger women as workers at home (NASB), or keepers at home (KJV). Thus, the ideal for women—whether they end up single or married—involves developing skills and entrepreneurial ventures, rather than aiming for a college degree that results in a job outside the home.

Therefore, a college education does not provide the most advantageous type of higher education for a woman. Andelin observes:

> It doesn't seem logical for a woman to train for a career in the event of widowhood or a rare emergency, if by so doing she bypasses a rich cultural education which would make her a better wife and mother. A man may as well train for motherhood and homemaking if this logic is sound.[7]

Unhelpful College Habit #5: Independence

College life fosters the unfeminine habit of operating with a spirit of independence. For at least four years, young ladies experience the freedom of planning their own daily schedule without having to run decisions by anyone else. Many a woman has commented later in life that this taste of independence eventually brought internal chafing when she sought to submit as a married wife.

The idea of it being a good thing to live independently is unrealistic. All throughout life, people are designed to operate as part of a family—adapting to others' needs, running decisions through authority structures, etc. Thus, the habit of learning to be completely independent is not as helpful as it first appears.

(Note: independence is different from competency, as Jasmine Baucham points out in her book, *Joyfully at Home*: "A suitable helper should be one of the most competent, intelligent, and driven women around."[8] Competency is a good thing when it is placed under the understanding that God has designed individuals to operate within the protective interconnectivity of an authority structure, rather than independently.)

The appeal to launch into a career that is not based at home pulls strongly on young women, but "the hard reality is that their goals may change the moment they hold their firstborn child in their arms. Suddenly their priorities shift and they want to raise their own children, not hire a nanny. Career ambitions can go away; but student loan debt is forever."[9] So stated an insightful mother in an article entitled "A College Degree? Not for My Kid." The time to think about what route will best equip one for life as a woman is before paying a penny for a degree that might do just the opposite.

As a Talented Individual

Finally, after determining what it means to work as a Christian, and which roles God has designed or not designed for women, we can now assess our unique skills and how they fit into finding the optimum vocation. The Creator "wired" each of us to enjoy doing different kinds of work so that through people working together—each in a role they like best—every necessary job would get done. Understanding this, the challenge becomes one of identifying our individual wiring and the vocation that best fits it. The Heavenly Father gives us clues about what He designed us to do; pulling those clues together helps to solve the vocational puzzle one piece at a time until the whole picture of our design comes into focus.

So, begin compiling your clues. Write down a list of activities that you are good at doing. Perhaps you can make time to do this right now, stopping intermittently to think and write while reading on... Your list could include skills such as sewing, administration, growing a garden, organizing a closet, etc. Ask your family what *they* think your unique talents are. Pencil the skill down, no matter how miniscule it is, even if you cannot yet see how it could become a vocation.

To help prompt your memory, think back to the "let's pretend" activities you loved to play over and over as a child. Were you a busy secretary with delightfully messy papers scattered about your toy typewriter? Maybe you gathered the neighborhood children to rows of desks and taught them school. Perhaps your favorite pastime involved sorting and organizing things. Did you love nursing injured little pets and wild animals? Or maybe you were the people-person of the family, who enjoyed taking imaginary (and real) phone calls, and scheduling social events. Each of these childhood attractions reveals something regarding the vocation God designed for you.

Your God-given wiring also shows forth in what responsibilities you gravitate toward in a group project. A secretarial-type person wants to manage the check-in table, while a visionary finds a way to end up leading the group, and a people-person volunteers to make nametags for everyone.

Ask yourself, do I like working with people, ideas, or things? All vocations can basically be sorted into those three categories. Individuals who thrive on working with people will find themselves extremely frustrated if they have to fix widgets in isolation. And people who love organizing things will become exhausted if forced to generate new ideas for a brainstorming project. So, it is helpful to know which type of work you prefer. Then you know what vocational opportunities to say no to right up front, because you recognize that they are not positions that would allow you to thrive.

John Stonestreet, speaker at Summit Ministries, suggests three thought-provoking questions for finding one's life purpose. They are as follows:

1. What can you not, *not* do?

    (Keep in mind that often the very activities we think we can "not *not* do" the Heavenly Father in His loving wisdom asks us to lay on the altar. Sometimes, this "Abraham offering Isaac" test ends with the Lord restoring that Isaac in a newly consecrated way. The Almighty can better use the work we love to do once we have surrendered it fully to His Lordship.)

2. What gives you the most satisfaction?

    (When you do it you really feel like "that's me at my ultimate." Eric Liddell—whose life story has become a favorite through the film *Chariots of Fire*—expressed it for himself when he said, "When I run I feel God's pleasure.")

3. What breaks your heart?

    (We work most vibrantly on needs that pull compassion from our heart. Discovering what breaks our heart helps us to see what work motivates us most.)

Your unique strengths do not automatically dictate that you should follow them all to their highest potential. For instance, Albert Schweitzer was expected to continue professionally as an organist on the great stages of Europe. He was an expert on interpreting Bach's compositions.

However, Schweitzer's greater life mission was his invaluable humanitarian work in Africa. For his musical talent to have remained in the limelight of cultured gentility would have meant that Africa would have lacked the leper colony and hospital which he founded, and he probably would not have won a Nobel Peace Prize. As it turned out, playing a second-rate organ in the huts of Africa gave him needed refreshment from his hospital work, even though he did not have the opportunity to perform frequently for sophisticated appreciative audiences.

Eric Liddell's life reveals the same principle. Though he knew God had created him to run, he also knew that his entire life was not to be defined by running. After finishing as a gold medalist in the 1924 Olympics, he headed to China as a missionary, and ended up giving his life for the Chinese people. Eric Liddell knew better than to limit his whole life focus to revolve around his talent as a runner.

So, be sure to listen to the Creator's leading as to what degree of importance your talent should hold in your life. As His people, we are called first to be faithful to Him, then to the destiny of our gender (women to be nurturers in the home), and only then to blossom in our specific area of talent. Talent has to defer to serving the Creator and fulfilling our design as women. People around you will encourage you to go to the top with your talent, but perhaps you were not meant to in that particular arena. Every ocean has its shore.

Those at the top of your field of talent cannot bless your neighbors and family; you can. You can reach people who the Greats cannot. By doing so, even in obscurity, you make a difference that would not be made without you.

As they say in photography, others would travel miles and miles to photograph scenes that are everyday sights for you. So, do not feel like you have to go abroad to make an impact; use your skill to minister to those close by you. Right where you are, your talent can be a blessing.

"Genius is 1% inspiration and 99% perspiration" as Albert Einstein noted (and he would know). So, don't wait for talent to carry you to a dream destination. Work diligently within every realm of responsibility, because "in all labor there is profit, but mere talk leads only to poverty" (Proverbs 14:23 NASB). While identifying one's talents can help impart clarity of direction, it is important to put them to use in every *present* circumstance, instead of waiting for and talking about an *optimal* work arena that may never arrive.

Education to Sharpen Talent

Trade schools offer a great alternative to college for guys, and why not for us ladies as well? The difference between a trade school (or a short, intensive workshop) and college is that the focus remains directly on the skill, and more godless general educational courses are not required.

Those who have an interest in cooking could take a culinary course. There are many culinary schools and seminars throughout the country that specialize in gourmet, raw, or just all-around-yummy cooking.

Others will want to improve their sewing skill, or learn how to sew, period. Weeklong sewing workshops are held around the country. Find an experienced seamstress through sewing how-to books in the library and check online to see if the author holds workshops.

Some would love to learn photography techniques. One such privately-run Christian photography school is the Institute of Photographic Studies.*

Trade workshops and institutes can be a great way to refine needed vocational skills without forfeiting large amounts of time, excessive money, and precious moral purity in the process.

Skills Everyone Needs

There are some skills that a girl simply needs to master, whether or not she has a natural affinity for them, because of the likelihood that she will be managing a home someday. Ideally, each young person should spend some specialized time in his or her mid to late teens focusing on areas in which it would benefit *everyone* to develop general competency. This plan would resemble an apprenticeship, except time with each skilled teacher would be limited to a month instead of several years.

Think of adults you know (preferably believers) who are experts in each of the areas listed below, and then approach them, offering free labor in exchange for their helping you develop your skills. Tell them, "I am a willing, hard worker, eager to watch you and pitch in where I can."

---

* For more information, see: www.ipsphoto.co.

Imagine how beneficial it would be for young men to apprentice for a month in each of these areas:

- ❖ Carpentry
- ❖ Electrical Wiring
- ❖ Plumbing
- ❖ Auto Mechanics
- ❖ Shooting
- ❖ CPR/First Aid

And it would also be invaluable for young women to find older women with whom to spend a month mastering:

- ❖ Cooking

  (Find professional cooks whose meals taste amazing, and spend time in their kitchens, chopping food for them as they share their tasty and timesaving secrets. Maybe you would want to spend a week each on four different ethnicities— perhaps in restaurants or simply with local homemakers from different countries who have a special knack at making really tasty meals. Make it a goal to conquer seven favorite dinners by the end of this month. Cook them over and over until they are no longer a challenge. When you are expecting your first baby, you will be grateful not to have to learn how to cook *then* with morning sickness clouding your mind.)

- ❖ Sewing/Tailoring

  (Become capable of sewing clothes and mending and altering them for your family. You might have to pay for sewing lessons, unless the seamstress has parts of projects with which she would not mind you helping her as she teaches you.)

❖ Hospitality

(Serve at a bed and breakfast or other hospitality center such as one that houses missionaries on furlough. Learn skills from hostesses who are known for making people feel at home.)

❖ Babysitting

(Offer to care for a busy mother's baby while she is right there, asking her to give you input on how to improve your baby skills, and showing you the best ways to change a diaper and bathe a newborn. Or volunteer in an orphanage overseas. Feeling competent and not overwhelmed with babies is the aim. The more time you take care of a baby, the more intuition you will develop. You will grow to have more accurate guesses of exactly why a baby is crying, and what he or she needs. You will glean invaluable tips along the way from experienced mothers that will equip you for your own motherhood adventure someday.)

❖ CPR/First Aid

(Take a quick training course in your area—they can be located online.)

If you are beyond your late teens and still do not feel competent in some of these areas, it is not too late. Set aside time to invest in developing these skills.* You will never regret doing so. Proficiency in these areas will assist

---

* For an extended list of such skills, see the *Godly Daughter Checklist* available at www.homeschoolhowtos.com.

you your whole life long, as you become the head and not the tail. Wherever you go in life, if someone needs a button sewn on their clothes, you will know how; or if a large family needs someone to come cook for them after the birth of a new baby they will know you can handle the challenge; or if a mother needs a break from a crying baby, you will have "itching arms" to take over. Conversely, young women who have not worked to acquire these feminine skills will not be able to take charge when needs arise. Your skills prepare a place for you.

Putting the Three Together

We have now seen how running vocational possibilities through these three filters to find an optimal vocational match makes the process much less vague. As the saying goes, more information always makes a decision for you.

So, now that you are on your way to discovering what vocations are fitting for a Christian woman with your talents, the question remains: How does a girl train for her vocation without being corrupted through college? Is it even possible to receive necessary training without college?

Start by finding a professional in the field that you are interested in pursuing and ask to be able to shadow him or her for a day. You will learn more from seeing what the job actually entails than from reading any number of career description books. One girl who did not do this thought she wanted to be a veterinarian. She went through eight years of veterinarian schooling and finished her degree only to find out that she could not handle putting animals "down," which turned out to be a large percentage of the job. Watching a veterinarian work for just a day *first* would have revealed to her how often the job involved putting animals down. It would have saved her from going into debt for a hundred-thousand-dollar degree that she didn't want.

A True Story of a Useless Degree

After graduating college, one young person "applied for a job at McDonald's. Under 'educational experience,' the individual listed a 6-year degree in Calligraphy. The [co-workers] hung the application on the wall and had quite a few chuckles. They laughed because the degree was absurd and stereotypical. ... Spending $50,000 [for it] was probably a bad choice. The individual could have simply learned the trade without the degree, and saved thousands."[10]

Also, think outside the box as far as working from home. The world would like us to think that we cannot make money or have a business from the "limitation" of a home setting, but this is not true. Perhaps instead of getting a degree in massage therapy, for example, a young lady could apprentice from a woman who is an excellent Christian massage therapist, and just learn massage techniques without getting certified. She could not legally charge for massages without certification, but she could offer her services on a donation basis and make almost as much without having to go through massage school. She could provide massages at her home or at Christian ladies' retreats with a sign displaying a suggested donation. This way, she might actually come out ahead financially, without having to pay back the thousands of dollars that massage school would cost. Likewise with many other occupations, ways to work from home can be developed with a little ingenuity.

Similarly, it is possible to sidestep being required to have a degree in order to work in a vocation. A doctor, for instance, needs a degree in order to practice medicine in most countries. But a gal might decide that she would rather not become an M.D., but simply acquire medical proficiency in order to serve in an underdeveloped country. To help the sick as a missionary overseas, a person needs skills, not necessarily a degree.

So, think creatively to find some way outside the mainstream "degree-first" mentality. Remember that a degree is an arbitrary measure that may or may not prove a person's expertise as a worker. In the workplace, skills get people hired. After the Civil War, Booker T. Washington inspired the freed slaves by stating that a person with skills would be clamored for, regardless of his race. This is equally true in regard to accredited higher education. Skills are sought after, regardless (in many more cases than we generally admit) of whether they are accompanied by a degree. What client would turn a young lady down for not having a degree, if she shows him or her a portfolio of her top-notch work? After all, without the time absorption of college, it is possible to acquire four more years of life experience than peers who lose that time in sterile college classrooms.

Looking at those whom the Heavenly Father chose to be earthly parents for His Son reveals His mindset about people's value without traditional higher education. Mary and Joseph were not formally educated people—they were not a part of Gamaliel's household (Paul's scholarly teacher who was learned in the Torah). No, Joseph was just a humble, but skilled, carpenter. Yet, in God's estimation, entrusting His Son to those who had skills and character mattered more to Him than their lack of official education.

God values certain attributes higher than a college education, and the workplace does also. A degree has become only an item to be checked off on an application so employers can move on to analyzing whether the applicant has skills and real-life experience. One college student was asked to sort job applications as a part of her internship. Her boss asked her to put the applications from people with master's degree who did not have much life experience on the bottom of the stack and the applications from people with the most experience on the top, even if they did not have a degree. That assignment opened her eyes to realize what was of true value to an employer. Colleges claim that a degree is of the utmost importance, but the real world wants skills and competence.

Build a Resume

Sometimes it is beneficial to offer services to people for free, simply to build one's bank of experience. For example, if you are learning how to repair sewing machines, offer to fix your friends' machines for free. Or offer to intern for free for a month with some noble corporation. After a month, if you work hard, the people who have trained you will probably not want to let you go. But you can take the experience you have gained and make it work for you in a home-based business.

It is invaluable to obtain written references from those you have served. Make it your aim to collect a notebook of these references, which will greatly help when trying to contract future opportunities. Even if you never plan to do that specific type of work again, a reference that states something general about your work ethic, such as, "It was not only the way she worked, but the spirit with which she worked!" will be of great worth to you.

Ask for the written reference right after you are done with each job. Don't wait until you are trying to get another job to collect past references. Most of the time, busy people will prefer it if you create a draft for them to edit or sign. So, type up supportive comments that you have heard them say about your work. This way, you will be more likely to actually obtain the reference than if you ask a busy non-writer to compose something from a blank slate.

Then, when you are applying for a job, you can hand your potential client or employer a portfolio with samples of your work (if applicable), a resume listing all of your pertinent real-life experience, and several supportive letters of recommendation from happy clients. They will likely be so impressed as not to be concerned with whether or not you have a college degree. People who need a service or product will choose a capable person with experience over a college graduate with no experience.

Success Without College Testimony: Web Design

" The biggest factors for me in deciding not to go to college was the exorbitant expense and the low return value in my self-employed professional endeavors. That's not to say it would have been completely useless, but technology progresses at such a rapid pace that curriculums quickly become outdated. To make it worse, the fact that colleges require you to take classes that are completely irrelevant to your vocation is simply mind-boggling. In this day and age, if you're a driven individual, you can learn almost anything without a college handholding you through the process.

Ever since I was little, I've been fascinated with technology, especially computers. I love figuring out how things work, and as such, took apart many of my toys as I was growing up. So it was only natural that when our family got our first computer I tried to figure out how it worked as well. Sometimes my curiosity ended up in something not working as it should, but in time, I figured out enough to fix my own mistakes as I went along.

Then came the Internet, in a form of a 3.5-inch floppy disk labeled AOL 1.0. The web completely fascinated me. And over time, I figured out how to build a website of my own, complete with an animated American flag, copied from whitehouse.gov.

Years went by, and I continued to build personal websites for my friends and myself, learning as I went, until one day I was asked to build a site for a local business. This was my first paying job, and I took it very seriously. When the site was complete, the owner was thrilled. Time progressed, and I built some free websites for local non-profits, who in return, referred me to other businesses in need of websites.

Fast-forward to today, and I'm still building websites for businesses, however, my skill set has grown considerably since then, and as such, I'm continuing to push myself with bigger and more complex projects.

Since I don't have huge college loans to pay off, my expenses are quite low, so I'm able to offer my services at very competitive rates, which keep my satisfied customers coming back time and time again. As it stands today, I'm generally booked at least a month in advance, and have actually had to turn down some work, simply because there are not enough hours in the day. And in this economy, that's something I don't take for granted.

In my profession, success is about results, not a paper hanging on the wall. If I can properly assess a client's needs and build a working solution that solves their problems, I have a satisfied customer. When I work with other individuals, I don't ask to see a list of degrees, I ask to see a list of their actual work. Again, it's the end results (not degrees) that matter.

The key to success isn't college; it's learning how to learn. Do you know how to do something? Great, push yourself to do it even better, and once you've done that, learn how to do something new. There's no point in life where we simply arrive; life itself is a continual learning process. The only time we stop learning is when we stop living."

—JAY WILLIAMS, business owner of D3 Designs, thrilled husband (of Britney, p. 227), and father of two

CLEP Your Way to a Degree

If, after creatively brainstorming alternative ways to enter your vocational field, it becomes evident that there is no way to get past the requirement of a degree, then CLEPping out of courses can be a quick and affordable way to breeze through a significant portion of college. CLEP tests are a College Level Examination Program that offers a way to get college credit for studying material independently. This way it is possible to study largely from home and speed through without debt. This approach leaves more time and resources to move on to acquiring skill in the field.

One young lawyer has an incredible success story of getting his degree mostly through CLEP tests. At the age of seventeen, John Shea graduated with a bachelor's degree through CollegePlus! (a program that advises individuals through the CLEPping process). As soon as he graduated, he landed a job that paid $60,000 a year, and then went on to graduate school and became a lawyer at the age of twenty-one. Many others have similar success stories of spending half the time and a fraction of the money to obtain a degree through CLEP tests. For an excellent book on this college approach, read *College Without Compromise* by Scott & Kris Wightman.

There are several downsides to this option, however. Taking CLEP tests to get a degree should not be considered the equivalent of gaining a higher *education*. Rather, CLEP provides a way to skim through the college system more quickly. The CLEP method of college embodies the ultimate "study for the exam" mentality. Since passing the test constitutes the ultimate goal of studying, critical thinking about content may give way to rote memorization. CLEPping out of courses does not differ from college studying in that regard; thus, it may not provide as thorough an education as other alternatives.

The ethical dilemmas of college academics do not evaporate with CLEP tests, either—one still has to decide whether to answer test questions according to one's conscience or to choose the answer necessary for a good grade. The biology CLEP test is a prime example of this, because of its focus on evolution. Answering "incorrectly" according to the evolutionist test writers may result in failing the test; so the question remains: Is obtaining a degree worth the necessary compromise? Also, most colleges only allow around half of a student's credits to be filled through CLEP tests, so it is necessary to finish one's degree either online or at a physical campus—and thus be immersed in all the traditional vortexes of college life that one was trying to avoid. Therefore, it is probably not worth pursuing the avenue of CLEPping for a degree that does not bring a vocation close on its heels.

CLEP only diminishes the problems of going through college—it does not eliminate them. Sometimes opportunities arise and pursuing them makes more sense than taking the time to get a degree. If there is a way to prepare for a vocation without college, so much the better.

Vocational Vision

Through this chapter, it has become evident that following God's calling to a noble occupation may involve sacrifice. Preparation for a vocation may also take some maneuvering to accomplish without the corruption of college; but it can be done. Many paths, including apprenticeships, trade schools, and independent skill building—not just college—can adequately equip a person for their life vocation.

No-degree Testimony: Success with Technology

" I have no regrets about not getting a college degree. I really don't think that I would be more successful if I had one, because I know people with degrees who have not made it as far up the corporate ladder as I have. Ever since my wife and I got married in 1994, she has not had to work a single day. We asked the Lord to provide a way for her to stay home with our kids and homeschool, and He has faithfully done so.

Growing up, my family was quite poor (I was the oldest of eight kids on a barber's salary), but today, I work for one of the fastest growing companies in the country. Our customers are some of the largest companies in the US, and at the rate we are growing, I expect we'll hit $1 billion in revenue in the next five years. I am a part of the leadership team and am well respected in terms of my vision and ability to clearly articulate the value of the services we provide to our customers. I have seven people reporting to me and I report directly to the senior vice president of worldwide sales. Since 1999, I have not made under $100,000 annually (except for one year).

I don't think parents and kids should assume college is the only option for them after they complete school. I'm convinced the quality of a college education does not match the cost. College is where many Christians walk away from the Lord because their faith is attacked nonstop.

My recommendation to young people is to work hard in every job with the goal of asking your employer for a letter of recommendation when you leave. Never burn bridges and always look for ways to take on more responsibility in your position. Without a degree, you have to show you have experience.

Sometimes the best way to advance and give yourself a raise is by changing companies. It's always easier to get a job if you already have a job. Embrace and enjoy interviewing. Always be well prepared, dress well, take notes, ask lots of questions, and send thank you notes (or emails) afterwards. You've got to set yourself apart from the rest of the interviewees.

I think parents and kids really need to consider what God has planned for them after graduating instead of assuming college is a requirement for their life to be successful. My story is proof that you can find success without a degree."

—GARTH OLIVERIA, husband and father of three,
Director of Business Development for
an information security company

8

AN EXCEPTIONAL EDUCATION

"Study to show yourself approved unto God."
(2 Timothy 2:15 KJV)

"We are addicted to schooling and we are ignorant about education." So observed Voddie Baucham, a dynamic Christian speaker, regarding our contemporary culture's view of college. Universities have gotten sidetracked from their primary purpose of educating young people; now they just shuttle them through the schooling system. College is no longer a place to go to cultivate one's mental acuity, but rather a place to be indoctrinated against one's core beliefs.

At the time the first universities were founded in America, books in vast quantities were not yet widely available to the common man. Therefore, universities used to be essential places to advance one's education because of the great repositories of books available in their libraries.

This scarcity of books was also the motivating reason behind the archaic need for classroom lectures, as an article in *The Atlantic* revealed:

> "Lectures came about several hundred years ago when there was one copy of the book, and the only person who had it was the professor[.] The only way to convey the content was for the professor to stand at the front of the room and read the book. One would hope that we had better capabilities these days."[1]

We currently have far more information at our fingertips through the Internet than the greatest university library ever contained. Therefore, the need to be physically present at a university in order to continue one's education has dwindled over the years.

However, with progress of technology being so gradual, many have been imperceptive to the change and do not realize that now, independent learning may be a far better option for higher education than college. The new online learning opportunities that emerge every few months are so groundbreaking that their potential could eventually shift the foundation of collegiate schooling.

Thus, we do not need to remain in the brick and mortar college setting in order to gain an exceptional education. Colleges are doing such a poor job at education that a person can learn more applicable knowledge outside of college without even exerting effort, simply through immersion in real life. So, whatever education we intentionally pursue beyond removing ourselves from the college unreality bubble is bonus.

Though leaving college can be a step in the right direction for many, it is of great importance to take a further step and make it a priority to educate our minds beyond the specifics needed for a vocation. We have a responsibility as believers created in the image of God to "study to show [ourselves] approved unto God." His people are meant to be the head and not the tail, to be examples and not warnings, and to bring glory to Him through being educated rather than derelict.

As dominion takers in this world (see Genesis 1:28), we have the responsibility to cultivate our mental soil in order to be better ambassadors for the Heavenly King. We want to be ambassadors whom the world respects because of our skills and knowledge, not slobs whom the world despises and considers not worth the time to listen to. Education generates respect, and that is what we are after, not only for ourselves, but also for the causes for which we stand. If we want to lead people, it is vital to first gain their respect.

Seeking education beyond the elementary basics results in becoming a broader person. A liberal education— one that broadens a person's general knowledge (as opposed to specific vocation-related knowledge)—enables a person to further marvel at the Creator's handiwork, and increases one's desire to worship. Higher education also continues to stretch the brain by laying down new neuron pathways, networking the brain into more of an interconnected, quick-functioning asset. Thus, acquiring an extensive knowledge base of concepts (even if they may not seem directly applicable to one's life) is a pursuit of immense value.

An excellent broad advanced education can be most advantageously brought about through diligent personal study, rather than in a classroom setting such as college. Christopher Lasch stated, "Mass education ... is intrinsically incompatible with the maintenance of educational quality."[2] At college, students are uniformly inculcated with liberal ideology and simultaneously discouraged from thinking for themselves as individuals. Therefore, quality education is best "accomplished through mentorship or apprentice-like interactions between a learner and an expert. Paper textbooks, 50-minute monologues, and passive learning are on the way out."[3] Surprisingly, this quote came from the mouth of a past professor at MIT— Woddie Flowers. Even *he* realized, as he looked back on the university situation, that college is not the optimum environment for an exceptional education.

Through independent study rather than cookie-cutter schooling, it is possible to go at one's own pace, and also to invest additional time on areas of particular interest. This can be done throughout a lifetime, but the young-adult years are an optimal time to establish a substantial foundation—as universities have capitalized upon. Individuals will never again have so much freedom of time at their disposal as they do as a young adult. Marriage, vocations and other responsibilities will increasingly infringe upon any hours one might like to spend on the development of the mind. So it is vital to diligently redeem the time by pursuing a better liberal education than can be gained through college.

Amy Carmichael, the missionary who founded the Dohnavur orphanage in India and wrote thirty-seven books, once observed about her own life's preparation, "Home, with all its prohibitions and opportunities to die daily"[4] offered training far greater than any Bible school curriculum. And author Jennie Chancey notes, "The stay-at-home daughters who come out of [formal] schooling and know that education is everywhere at their fingertips are the ones that are excelling." Let us aim to be that type of daughters as we each diligently pursue unique avenues of higher education from home.

The Power of Small Moments

One of the chief challenges of pursuing an education outside the framework of college is discipline. Putting off the cultivation of the mind until "some day" is the equivalent of never making it happen. An education is something to go after doggedly in small moments, day after day. The chunk of time you think you need in order to read an intellectual book or write a research paper will not arrive on an empty platter with nothing else vying for its attention. The only way to find time for independent education is to set one's will to devote a certain reasonable amount of time to it per day, and also to marshal every small moment for the cause.

An old inspiring story of a medical student exemplifies the value of using small moments wisely. This student, whom we will call Bill, along with his acquaintances, had fifteen spare minutes after their last class, before dinner each evening. They regularly spent this time aimlessly discussing happenings from the day. Often one or the other of the students would point out the large medical encyclopedia that sat on the coffee table in the midst of their waiting room and comment on how he wished he would be able to find time to read it someday.

Unlike the others, Bill decided to do something proactively to accomplish his desire: he committed to read the book in those spare minutes before dinner each afternoon. In this way he found exactly five hours a month to progress through the book. Bill faithfully kept his focus, to the exclusion of time-wasting chatter with his peers, and in two years time, he closed the book, gave it a sound pat, and turned to his friends. "Well, chaps, I have just completed reading every page of that marvelous book." They could not believe it. While they waited for an opportune block of time that never came, Bill had put his small moments to good use.

The cumulative advantage of just fifteen minutes daily advanced Bill ahead of those who wasted that time. It will do the same for each of us who take advantage of our free moments. We cannot create more time, but we can diligently take advantage of our free moments by always having a book, a card of memory work, or a pad of paper on hand, "redeeming the time" (Ephesians 5:16) at every opportunity.

You will be amazed at how much can be accomplished in a focused fifteen minute period. Set a timer sometime to convince yourself of the efficacy of small moments. A person can actually accomplish far more in a short length of focused time than in a longer length of time with diffused concentration.

An Educational Plan

So, what does the framework of an independently-gained education look like? Intentional reading, critical writing, attending seminars, taking online courses, and one-on-one private lessons can all play a part in the process of attaining an exceptional education.

Try to devote two hours each day to the advancement of your mind. This time can be found by closing that Facebook account and signing out of instant messaging. Some find it helpful to schedule their time on the Internet and set a timer to keep it to the allotted time (or download a free computer software such as SelfControl that blocks access to the Internet for a set amount of time). Maybe you decide that you can afford to spend fifteen minutes in the morning and fifteen minutes at night online. To help you succeed in your resolve, keep a running list of things you would like to look up whenever you would normally turn straight to the Internet to do so. You will find that this focuses your Internet time and allows you to be more productive with long-term goals the rest of the day.

Disciplining and stretching one's mind must take a place of high importance in order for a person to succeed at gaining a broad advanced education on their own. In one year, the difference will be very noticeable between someone who has ordered their time to make education a priority and someone who has frittered away their time.

Now let's delve into some specifics of how to go about obtaining an advanced education.

Reading

You can shape your future self by choosing what books you read. The best leaders were first readers. This is because through reading, a person can glean from the wisdom and knowledge of the ages, absorbing in a matter of hours another person's condensed lifetime's work.

People can be classified either as literate, illiterate, or as part of the new popular class of people: the aliterate. Literates can read; illiterates can't read; and aliterates refuse to read, though they are able to read. Not reading may seem like the easier way to live, but aliterates do not realize that as a result of their choice to turn a cold shoulder to books, they will become followers by default, rather than leaders. Consequently, they become susceptible to whatever the media wants them to believe, because they lack an educated literary background and a cultivated logic that would aid them in analyzing what they are told. Want to lead? Then pull a book off the shelf and read.

Stretch yourself by reading books that are just a bit challenging, rather than only pleasurable, easy reads. Reading just above one's comfort level is the way to grow.

Start compiling a reading list that covers a broad variety of subjects. Ask older people who are well read and who know you well to recommend life-changing books. Tell them that you desire to be stretched mentally, so any title is fair game. Perhaps you will end up reading about the eye-opening history of feminism, or the invention of the camera-inside-a-pill that takes 50,000 pictures during its journey through a patient's digestive tract, or the biography of a midwife, or the miraculous history of the nation of Israel. Even consider plunging into recommended books in which you are not especially interested, to expand yourself for a few chapters. Interlibrary loan can become a best friend, bringing you books that you may only read once and do not need to purchase.

Here is a sample of some highly recommended books:

Spiritual:

- ❏ *Paradise Lost*, John Milton
- ❏ *Gaining Favor with God and Man*, Mantle Ministries (1800's anecdotal essays on character)
- ❏ *God's Mighty Hand*, Richard "Little Bear" Wheeler (historical stories involving Providence)
- ❏ *Half Hour Talks on Character Building by Self-Made Men and Women*, edited by J. S. Kirtley
- ❏ *Equipped to Love*, Norm Wakefield
- ❏ *The Purity Principle*, Randy Alcorn
- ❏ *I Kissed Dating Goodbye*, Joshua Harris
- ❏ *Mere Christianity*, C. S. Lewis
- ❏ *This Present Darkness*, Frank Peretti (fiction)
- ❏ *Safely Home*, Randy Alcorn (fiction)

Femininity:

- ❏ *How to be A Lady*, Harvey Newcomb (1862)
- ❏ *It's (Not That) Complicated: How to Relate to Guys in a Healthy, Sane, and Biblical Way*, Anna Sofia & Elizabeth Botkin
- ❏ *Preparing to be a Help Meet*, Debi Pearl

- ❑ *Passionate Housewives Desperate for God*, Jennie Chancey and Stacy McDonald (about turning from the feminist deception)

Classics:
- ❑ *Dr. Jekyll and Mr. Hyde*, Robert Lewis Stevenson
- ❑ *A Tale of Two Cities*, Charles Dickens
- ❑ *The Robe*, Lloyd C. Douglas
- ❑ *Ben Hur*, Lew. Wallace
- ❑ *Uncle Tom's Cabin*, Harriet Beecher Stowe

Biographies: (It is tragic for any believer not to know the legacies left by each of these trailblazers.)
- ❑ *Bonhoeffer: Pastor, Martyr, Prophet, Spy*, Eric Metaxas
- ❑ *Ten P's in a Pod*, Arnold Pent III (the first modern homeschool family; they memorized the Bible)
- ❑ *Tongue of the Prophets*, Robert St. John (the man who revived Hebrew from being a dead language)
- ❑ *Hudson Taylor's Spiritual Secret*, Dr. and Mrs. Howard Taylor
- ❑ *The Hiding Place*, Corrie ten Boom
- ❑ *Through Gates of Splendor*, Elisabeth Elliot
- ❑ *George Mueller*, Faith Coxe Bailey
- ❑ *Gladys Alward: The Little Woman*, Gladys Alward
- ❑ *A Chance to Die: The Life and Legacy of Amy Carmichael*, Elisabeth Elliot

Self-Help:

❏ *How to Win Friends and Influence People*, by Dale Carnegie

Reading voraciously does not automatically translate to having a well-educated mind. Education takes place as the mind develops acumen through thinking critically about what one has read. Isaac Watts, writer of approximately six hundred profound hymns, commented on the need to reach beyond simply reading. He wrote:

> A well-furnished library and a capacious memory are indeed of singular [exceptionally good] use toward the improvement of the mind; but *if all of your learning be nothing else but a mere amassment of what others have written, without a due penetration of their meaning, and without a judicious [evaluation] and determination of your own sentiments,* I do not see what title your head has to true learning above your shelves ... With the neglect of your reasoning powers, you can justly claim no higher character but that of a good historian."[5]

So, aim to be more than a book-wormish receptacle of information. Sharpen your mind through critical thinking about what you read. A good way to do this is to write responses to books. Writing is a "discipline which calls into exercise the intellectual faculties, and enables us to employ them in the investigation of the truth. This discipline is a necessary preparation for profitable reading."[6]

Read stimulating non-fiction books, and interact with the text by writing down concepts that you want to mull over or write another opinion about later. Take the time to look up the meaning of unfamiliar words, and enlarge your vocabulary by writing down new words in order to review them periodically to see if you remember how to use them in a sentence.

Writing

Francis Bacon observed, "Reading makes a full man, conversation a ready man, and writing an exact man." Therefore, when reading, pause to ask questions such as, "Do I agree with that? Why or why not?" and then write a few paragraphs in response. When you finish a biography, don't just put it on the shelf. Challenge yourself to write a position paper in response to what you have read. Writing helps one to clarify vague convictions on topics. For example, after reading a biography about Bonhoeffer, a reader could write about whether she thinks it was right for him, as a pacifist, to be involved in the conspiracy to assassinate Hitler. Come up with topics of response for each book you read. Exerting discipline to take the time to think, and to think well through writing, begins to shape clarity out of mental mush.

As Harvey Newcomb advised young ladies in 1851:

I know of nothing which more effectually calls out the resources of the mind than writing. To a person unaccustomed to this exercise, it appears exceedingly difficult. But a little practice will make it a pleasing and delightful employment. The mind is far more richly feasted with ideas conceived and brought forth by itself, than by those produced by others, and communicated through the medium of the senses; and all the intellectual faculties are strengthened and improved by exertion.[7]

... Do not indulge the absurd notion that you can write only when you feel like it. Remember your object is to discipline the mind, and bring it under the control of the will. But, to suffer your mind to be controlled by your feelings, in the very act of discipline, is absurd. As well might a mother talk of governing her child, while she allows it to do as it pleases.[8]

After writing a position paper, be sure to share it with good writers for their input. Your editor could be an aunt, or a woman in your community, or even one of your own parents. Ask him or her to read your paper and mark it with constructive criticism. This editing process will be painful, but incredibly revealing. A writer can think something makes sense, but hearing from an objective reader as to whether or not it actually *does* is a different matter. After receiving feedback, take the comments and re-work your paper. Tweak the words and content, until you feel that your writing is as clear and aptly worded as possible. Refer to a thesaurus to discover alternative, more descriptive words to incorporate. Stronger writing avoids using "be" verbs such as: is, was, were, am, etc. whenever possible, and integrates more descriptive action verbs instead.

Also, avoid using "I" or "you" in most writing. For example, the sentence, "I thought that Bonhoeffer was a great theologian," could be improved by stating the fact and then giving reasons to back it up, like this: "Bonhoeffer's reputation as a great theologian resulted from his disciplined, studious habits." Notice, also, that the more descriptive verb "resulted" replaces "was." Though a painful process at first, editing grows more and more intriguing as your skill in the hunt for better phrasing improves.

Another way to exercise mental muscle would be to write up spiritual encouragements for other young ladies. There are plenty of godly-girlhood magazines in circulation that need well-written inspirational articles. You are almost guaranteed to have an article published in one of them. Keep a record of what article was published in what magazine, and the date of the issue. This may come in useful for referencing on a resume someday if you want to apply for a contracted writing job (perhaps from home).

You may feel like you are not gifted at writing. If so, remember that the point of making the effort to write is your own educational *improvement*, and though "it is true some possess talents of a superior order; ... none, except idiots, are incapable of improvement"[9] as Harvey Newcomb wittily encouraged in the 1800's. You do not have to start out as a good writer in order to sharpen your thinking skills through writing. Just the process of attempting to put thoughts down on paper in a concrete form will cause you to have to think much more critically, and will provide you with an exceptional education.

Success Without College: Published Author

Even though Sarah Mally (33) does not have a college degree, she has become a successful author and has been able to pour herself into founding a discipleship ministry that now has 500 groups worldwide. When she graduated from high school, she did not sense the Lord calling her to go to college, but rather to focus on Bright Lights—her program for young ladies.

When she turned twenty, a friend encouraged her to go to Bible college, but she realized that she did not have to be at a Bible college in order to study the Bible. She realized that additional studies could be coordinated from home and that God could continue to prepare her in other ways. The Lord gradually led her to decide not to pursue a degree as she sensed her responsibility to invest in the ministries the Lord had already given her.

Sarah is thankful that the Lord led her to stay home. He gave her many unique opportunities to learn and gain experiences, which she believes surpass the prospects available at college. As she points out, students spend a lot of time writing in college, but they usually have to write assignments that they are not personally passionate about. By writing without college constrictions, Sarah was freed up to coauthor *Making Brothers and Sisters Best Friends*, and also to author *Before You Meet Prince Charming* (each of which has sold over 50,000 copies).

Spelling

What do you atomatikaly tend to think of a person who rites with glaring misspelings sprinkeled throughout there centences? That they are not very well educated, right? Spelling is a prominent mark of education that many knowingly or unknowingly take note of in an evaluation of whether or not what someone has written is worth attention.

As leaders-to-be, we need to make it a priority to spell correctly. We may think we can depend on Spell Check to save us from mortification, but how much better to aim to master spelling without that crutch? How much consideration will a reader give an article if definitely is spelled "defiantly," or surely "surly"? Those transmuted words would have passed Spell-Check, but perhaps caused an important reader to stop heeding the author's argument. If a person cannot spell accurately, how are readers to trust in the accuracy of the *content* of her article?

We will always be learning new words, so mastering spelling will continually provide us with a challenge, but making the effort to meet it with competence will pay off. Memory hooks can integrate the right brain in the process, making spelling more fun and less effort. For example, take the word "accommodate." Picturing that a hotel room can accommodate two people in each bed helps one to remember to spell the word with two C's and two M's: accommodate. Or the mnemonic for remembering the two U's in "bouquet" could be imagining someone saying, "a bouquet for U, yes U!" With memory hooks, the struggle to spell these words vanishes, and likewise with every other word for which you invent a mnemonic. Continually adding to a list of words you have misspelled and creating memory hooks for them will greatly improve your spelling ability.

It might seem unnecessary to focus on spelling, but since it does offer such a visible manifestation of the quality of one's education, it is worth an investment of time. An important job application which contains one misspelled word could bring the interview process to as conclusive an end as just one wrong note in a professional musician's orchestral audition. Spelling is like good grooming; it informs other peoples' first impressions of you.

Misspelled words give the naysayers a chance to exclaim, "I told you so—it is impossible to get a good education outside of college—look at how poorly she spells." We must avoid the temptation to allow technology to make us dumber and dumber in spelling by depending on its aid. If we aim to have a strong testimony of how well a person can be educated without college, we need to make it a priority to spell correctly, even when Spell-Check is not available.

Online Opportunities

In addition to expanding the brain through independent reading and writing, online learning opportunities provide limitless possibilities for continuing one's education. Lovers of learning worldwide are beginning to become very excited at the thousands of top-notch courses available—many for free—over the Internet. The massive implications of the online higher education breakthrough that burgeons just around the corner should cause the trustees of brick and mortar universities to tremble at the implications. Free, extremely top-notch advanced educaι. n is now becoming available to anyone who wants to work for it.

Five hundred thousand engineering students in India are taking advantage of one example of such an online educational breakthrough. Because of the limited infrastructure in India, there was a great need for brilliant engineers-to-be to have a way to learn from home through the Internet. The National Programme on Technology Enhanced Learning (NPTEL) set out to meet that need, and simultaneously blessed the rest of the world with access to their courses as well. The NPTEL offers over 40 hours of lecture videos for each of over 120 courses in technology, engineering, science, mathematics, and more, on their website: www.nptel.iitm.ac.in.. The content is in English, and is available to anyone worldwide.

An even more exciting new development has entered the online learning arena thanks to Harvard and the Massachusetts Institute of Technology (MIT). Called edX, the non-profit venture was launched in the spring of 2012 with a pilot course on circuits and electronics. A group of 155,000 learners from 160 countries signed up for the course, which offered the same material as available on location at MIT (not a lite version of the course). Students who earned a passing grade (only 7,157, because of the level of rigor) received a certificate of mastery.

The greater-than-expected success of edX proves that this is the future of higher education. Young people worldwide are ready and eager to start learning at their own pace online. EdX aims to ultimately collaborate with other universities in order to provide a wide array of courses on a single website to learners anywhere there is an Internet connection. The online courses allow students to learn through video lesson segments, embedded quizzes, and online laboratories, and also offer opportunities to engage with professors and fellow classmates. EdX utilizes cutting-edge A/B testing where different students can get slightly different testing experiences tailored to their unique learning styles.

MIT itself has over 2,000 free OpenCourseWare courses with lecture notes, exams, and videos available to learners online at: www.ocw.mit.edu. These courses are on a broad range of topics, not just technology. Architecture, engineering, humanities, arts, social sciences, business management, and science courses cover the spectrum. MIT offers enough material on this website to provide a person with many years of study material.

Udacity is another growing, completely free online learning option for taking demanding courses online and augmenting one's independent learning. Udacity launched with an Artificial Intelligence Class in October of 2011. The enrollment for this course topped that of edX— 160,000 students from 190 countries. They learned how to program a robotic car right along with students at Stanford. A course on building a search engine followed as the next exciting opportunity. As of July 2012, Udacity offers around a dozen top-of-the-line courses in physics, business, computer science, statistics, and more.

Udacity's twenty-first-century university model offers courses taught by world-renowned university instructors through high-quality lecture videos that are less than five minutes long. Quizzes throughout measure comprehension of content. Students can sign up any time and complete the course at their own pace without deadlines for homework or quizzes. Final exams are offered every eight weeks, and a passing grade results in a certificate of completion. According to Udacity's website, their certificates "are recognized by major technology companies who are actively recruiting from the Udacity student body."[10] Udacity provides a great option for mathematically-minded learners (and others who simply want the challenge and educational exposure) to be stretched in their advanced education outside of college.

Of course, it is not yet possible to get a *degree* by independently studying free courses like these, but as we have already discussed, degrees are not a guarantee of future success anyway. The world is changing. Therefore, if what we are after is actual education rather than a piece of paper, these incredible online resources are available to use toward that end.

Of course, some colleges do offer accredited courses online to build up credit toward a degree if a person wants to pay the money. Either way—for credit or not—online education is better than what is offered at a physical university. Research done by the U.S. Department of Education involving over a thousand studies of online education has revealed that online learning situations "on average produce stronger student learning outcomes than do classes with solely face-to-face instruction."[11] Perhaps this is because "many college students snooze in big lecture halls. In good online courses, though, instructors require every student to answer questions and stay involved,"[12] according to an article in *World Magazine* entitled "Class Without Rooms."

Online courses mark the end of the need to leave one's home and move to college for four or more years to get an education. With these developments, there is no longer a need to attend a university, unless one's real reason for going to college is to get a diploma or to party.

Instructional Videos

Another way to build your own higher educational experience is to invite a world-class expert to lecture in your home through videos. Watch YouTubes or full multi-video sets to receive a focused, to-the-point education on a certain topic. Plenty of instructional videos can be located through Interlibrary loan on subjects such as public speaking, sewing, gardening, cooking, math, music, household repairs, and more. You name it; there is probably a video of an expert teaching it. Some specific video series recommendations are:

- ❏ Francis Schaeffer's *How Should We Then Live?*, (the classic 1976 series on the rise and decline of Western culture from a Christian perspective)
- ❏ *Leonard Bernstein's Young People's Concerts* with the New York Philharmonic (Kultur Video), (engaging classical music appreciation lectures interspersed with live symphonic examples)
- ❏ Jeff Meyer's *Secrets of Great Communicators*; *Secrets of World-Changers*; and *Secrets of Everyday Leaders* (B&H Publishing Group)

- ❒ *Moody Science Classics* (Moody Institute of Science) (episodes revealing the marvel of God's intricate design in science)
- ❒ *Sewing with Confidence* (www.u2cansew.com)
- ❒ *Homestead Blessings* with the West ladies (Franklin Springs Family Media). Includes: The Art of Bread Making, Cooking, Sewing, Quilting, Candle Making, Soap Making, Canning, Gardening, and Herbs

Music/Art

Taking lessons from terrific instructors across the country and practicing diligently has the potential to result in exceptional progress without weekly immersion in a liberal college music or art department. Even if a plane flights are necessary to reach master artists, such occasional lessons still cost less, overall, than college tuition.

Learn Another Language

People in other countries commonly speak three or four languages. In America we think that we are the most highly educated people in the world, yet the majority of us only speak one language. Studying another language not only equips us to better communicate with other people groups when traveling, but doing so also measurably sharpens cognitive skills. Researchers have found that students who studied a foreign language scored higher on multi-subject ACT and SAT tests,[13] and, incredibly, that "speaking two languages can help delay the onset of Alzheimer's symptoms by as much as five years."[14] Learning another language helps people adapt to change more easily, and makes them more cultured overall. So, foreign language is not an area that anyone should want to leave out of their exceptional education plan.

Many foreign language programs are designed for a person to be able to study on their own. Once you figure out what type of learner you are (visual, auditory, verbal, or tactile), then find the program that best fits that learning style (e.g. Rosetta Stone is more visual, Pimsleur is completely auditory, and a textbook—such as one that teaches verb conjugations—is verbal).

Be brave; dive right in to a language that you really want to learn. If you are motivated enough, you will not let anything hold you back. Set your sights high. Who said only seminary students could learn Hebrew, for instance?

Conferences, Seminars, and Workshops

Conferences are infinitely superior to college in that the finest speakers are brought together in one place for a short period of time. Colleges, on the other hand, often hire many mediocre professors to every one superb teacher. So, money invested in attending a conference yields far more than the same amount spent to attend college. At college, some teachers diffuse their course focus by talking off-topic since they know they have a lot of time to fill, while at a seminar, experts load every minute of their lectures with conceptual gems that leave a listener panting to take notes.

The benefit of short, succinct conferences is that they allow one to return to real life to test concepts right away (rather than forgetting them by waiting four years). Periodic intense learning through conventions, seminars, and conferences widens a person's horizons, and then real life solidifies the newly learned concepts.

Another advantage of conferences has to do with the type of people who attend. At conferences, attendees are usually adults, which relieves a dedicated person from having to endure immature and immoral lifestyles of other youth while focusing on learning. Moreover, no matter who the attendees are, they are motivated and have sacrificed to be there. The same cannot always be said about college students.

As the adage states, "Next year you will be the same person you are today except for the books you read and the people you meet." Where could one find a better place to network with choice people and discover new highly recommended resources than conferences? A week spent at a specialized conference results in invaluable exposure, learning, and personal contacts.

Summit Worldview Conferences

Summit Ministries provides excellent training for young people to master the core tenants of what they believe and why. Summit equips over fifteen hundred students ages sixteen and up every summer to be able to skillfully defend their faith. At its two-week conference, Summit teaches students how to think critically about cutting edge legal, psychological, sociological, and bioethical dilemmas. They study the six major worldviews in order to combat anti-biblical thought with razor-sharp logical skill.

Summit teachers have an exceptional expertise at training students how to think. Some of the professors act as "the devil's advocate," in order to challenge students to articulate their convictions. Whatever side of an argument a student takes, the professor might take the opposite stance, and by so doing, uncover the holes in the student's argument through the powerful Socratic method of questioning. This results in two weeks of some of the best education of one's life.

Whether a person plans to take even one college course, or launch into the business world, or become a mother to world-changers, two weeks at Summit is invaluable preparation to expertly handle every issue of life from a Christian perspective.*

An Occasional College Course

Chucking the college degree mentality does not necessarily imply that it is best *never* to take a college course. Perhaps one course with a superb teacher in graphic design or public speaking would be worth dipping into the college setting to obtain. At least then a young lady would be there for a course specifically targeted to what she wants, and not have to go through liberal general education requirements. Auditing a course for free may be a feasible option, too. However, be prepared to drop a class if it

---

* For more information, visit www.summit.org.

turns out to not be worth your while, or full of ungodly content.

Conclusion

The open doors to an exceptional education are many and varied. Do not let the absence of studying in a collegiate brick building deceive you into thinking you cannot learn great things another way. Realize, however, that when you are studying on your own, education will not automatically happen unless you set goals and exercise some will power to accomplish them.

So, pull out a pad of paper and start planning. If *you* were your academic advisor (and you are), what would you want to set down on that paper for your course of study over the next three months? List the books you want to have read in that time, the online courses you would like to take, the articles and essays you plan to write, the lessons for which to register, and the language program levels to complete. Then, weekly and monthly, refresh your goals and set deadlines for completing each baby step.

If you stay in the driver's seat, belted in with discipline, the road of your own exceptional education will take you on the journey of a lifetime. As Max Marmer, an entrepreneurial Stanford dropout says, "The best way to learn is through purpose-driven education. Taking classes in itself is worthless."[15]

No-Degree Testimony: Founded UnCollege, Winner of $100,000 Thiel Fellowship

"In elementary school, my parents allowed me to try ... home-schooling. While my peers sat in class through middle school and high school, I found mentors, took college classes, started businesses, lived in France, worked on political campaigns and helped build a library. I created my education by taking these traditional 'extra-curricular activities' and turning them into a cohesive academic program.

Although I never set foot in high school, I assumed college was the next step on my path to success. After all, my peers were all going to college, my parents had gone to college, and that's what society expected. I chose a private liberal arts college, Hendrix, which promised to change my life.

At college I saw professors researching, administrators building state-of-the-art facilities, and students partying. I found smart people with good ideas, but they were mostly just writing papers, not changing the world. College felt contrived, theoretical and irrelevant.

I started UnCollege.org early in my second semester to challenge the notion that college is the only path to success. It spread like wildfire. In late February, I told *New York Magazine* that I would leave school whether or not I got the Thiel fellowship. Two months later, I did.

Why did I make trouble? Going along with the program seems pretty sweet. I could have written papers, skipped class and partied until dawn. After four years as a college student, I would have had many friends, a good job and letters after my name. But I left college because I realized I couldn't rely on a university to give me an education."

—DALE STEPHENS (20), author of *Hacking Your Education* (Penguin: 2013), founder of UnCollege, $100,000 Thiel Fellowship winner (2011)

9

EXCELLING IN ENTREPRENEURSHIP

"She considers a field and buys it; from her profits she plants a vineyard. ... She makes linen garments and sells them, and supplies sashes for the merchants. ... Give her of the fruit of her hands, and let her own works praise her in the gates." (Proverbs 31:16, 24, 31)

How would you like to receive $100,000 to stop attending college and pursue entrepreneurship instead? Billionaire Peter Thiel (the first investor in Facebook, and cofounder of PayPal) offers just that through his "20 Under 20" fellowship program. Launched in 2011, the fellowship annually chooses 20 promising individuals under the age of 20 years old, awards each of them $100,000 to launch their entrepreneurial ventures, and mentors them with world-class leaders in Silicon Valley for two years.

Thiel (pronounced "teal") believes that higher education inhibits innovation, and student debt holds people back from launching entrepreneurial ideas. In a discussion about the total U.S. student debt of $1 trillion, he told CBS 60 Minutes, "That trillion dollars—want to describe it cynically? You can say it's paid for a trillion of lies about how good education is."[1] Therefore, winners of his $100,000 fellowship are required to stay out of college, except perhaps to audit a class directly pertinent to their field of interest. Thiel tells them, "waiting for graduation is an expensive waste of time."

Many of these fellowship winners already had their own businesses or were conducting lab research or had taught themselves computer programming when they were nine to thirteen years old! They are continuing on their way to success, and they are "stopping-out" (not dropping-out) of college, because college was impeding their individual goals with its finance-draining, time-absorbing requirements. None of these individuals *need* degrees as a prerequisite to success.

Notable 2011-2012 Thiel Fellows

Nick Cammarata (18) created Tablo, a tool for teachers to create lecture videos online that track students' progress. He "co-founded a file storage application that received 80 million visitors."[2]

Jim Danielson (20) is refining an electric motor he successfully designed and installed in a Porsche.

Laura Deming (17) is researching ways to extend human lifespans by a few centuries "at least," she says. She already has successfully extended the lifespans of worms in the laboratory.

Eden Full (19) invented a solar panel system that tracks with the sun and only costs $10. Eden's patent-pending SunSaluter currently provides power for two villages of 1,000 citizens in Kenya.

Kettner Griswold Jr. (20) designed antibiotic resistance counter-agents and spontaneous radiative thermal energy harvesting at room temperature. He is pursuing a revolutionary method of DNA synthesis.

Andrew Hsu (19) quit his fourth year as a neuro-science Ph.D. student at Stanford University to pursue his own Airy Labs.

Alexander Kiselev (19) is working to create affordable scientific instruments to be available to anyone who needs them.

Gary Kurek (19) invented a "walker-wheelchair hybrid that can provide power to assist its user according to how strong [he or] she feels at any moment."[3] Founder of GET Mobility Solutions.

David (Jiageng) Luan (19) "wants to create home robots that can handle an extensible array of low- to mid-level cognitive tasks in addition to physical jobs."[4]

John Marbach (17) aims to bring the classroom into the twenty-first century through Web-based videos and mobile apps. He created Glider, a Gmail plugin that sorts email by context.

Chris Olah (19) specializes in 3-D printing.

Dale Stephens (19) founded Uncollege and authored *Hacking Your Education,* a guide to gaining the skills colleges don't teach.

Charlie Stigler (19) wants to improve education by developing computer interfaces in teaching and coaching. He developed the SelfControl Mac application.

Sujay Tyle (17) was one of the youngest students at Harvard before he left in his junior year. He won the International Energy Olympiad award for his six years of research on converting cellulose to ethanol. "Named one of the Top Young Scientists across New York."[5]

Taylor Wilson (18) is an Applied Nuclear Physicist.

Ben Yu (19) climbed Mount Kilimanjaro and is working on "building an e-commerce start-up (Pricemash) that will revolutionize price comparison on the Web."[6]

Darren Zhu (19) is building "a diagnostic biosensor, the initial step toward making synthetic biology easier to engineer."[7]

The Thiel Fellows are examples of only some of the endeavors open to pursuit without a degree. Many more beckon. If a teenager can achieve nuclear fusion (as Taylor Wilson did at age fourteen) without having to go to college first, then that shatters the limitations we have put on ourselves. People who say a young person must get a degree in order to achieve success need to reconsider, because these Thiel Fellows are achieving success just fine without degrees. And they are not alone. Of the 2012 Thiel applicants, a thousand entrepreneurs remained beyond those who were selected as Fellows. Their desire to quit college to pursue businesses, inventions, and twenty-first-century advancements further proves how many individuals realize entrepreneurship may now be a better avenue to success than college.

Entrepreneurial Responsibility

Conversely, the vast majority of other young adults in this generation have become consumers rather than producers. Young people today would rather sit around and watch movies, waste time on the Internet, and go shopping, than discover the needs that exist in the world and then figure out how to meet them. Vanishing are those who finish a day of school and then vigorously turn their attention to developing entrepreneurial ventures in their basements. Youth now waste incredible amounts of "spare" time and end up with nothing to show for their hours by the time they reach full-bloomed adulthood.

Doug Phillips, in his Entrepreneurial Bootcamp introductory message, said, "It is a reproach on the body of Christ that we are a bunch of bored wastrels." He went on to state that the parable of the talents (see Matthew 25:14-30) teaches that every believer needs to operate with an entrepreneurial spirit, regardless of whether he or she is a business owner, an employee in someone else's business, or simply a family member. As servants of the King of the universe, we have a responsibility to be entrepreneurs, investing the talent He bestows. Phillips states: "entrepreneurialism is the moral obligation to be economically creative and productive." In the parable of the talents, entrepreneurs hear, "Well done, My good and faithful servant." Entrepreneurship pleases the King.

The Proverbs 31 Entrepreneur

For women, entrepreneurism is so much more ideal than working under the employment of men who are not their God-given authorities. As discussed in our earlier chapter on vocations, nowhere does Scripture mention an authority for a woman in addition to her father or husband. Attempting to be loyal to a boss and the man of her home can lead not only to conflict of direction, but also to divided affection. Women who work for men in the workplace become adept at meeting their bosses' quirky needs in a helpmate-like position. When the boss feels that his employee understands his needs better, the man's affection may begin to transfer from his wife to his helpmate-employee. Thus, working for other men is a hazardous "adultery minefield" best to be avoided if at all possible.

Point 14 of the "Tenets of Biblical Patriarchy" (a list of affirmations which describe the perspective of Doug Phillips of Vision Forum Ministries, Phil Lancaster of *Patriarch* magazine and R. C. Sproul, Jr., of the Highlands Study Center, among others) states:

> While unmarried women may have more flexibility in applying the principle that women were created for a domestic calling, it is not the ordinary and fitting role of women to work alongside men as their functional equals in public spheres of dominion."[8]

Scripturally, the roles that are exemplified involve women becoming entrepreneurially productive from home.

The Proverbs 31 woman certainly was an entrepreneur. As Matthew Henry wrote about her in his commentary:

> She applies herself to the business that is proper for her. It is not in a scholar's business, or statesman's business, or husbandman's business, that she employs herself, but in women's business ... she goes about it cheerfully and dexterously, lays not only her hand, but her mind to it, and goes on in it without weariness in well-doing.
>
> *She* also *plants a vineyard*, but it is *with the fruit of her hands*; she does not ... run into debt, to do it, but she does it with what she can spare out of the gains of her own housewifery. Men should not lay out any thing upon superfluities, till, by the blessing of God upon their industry, they have got before-hand, and can afford it; and *then* the fruit of the vineyard is likely to be doubly sweet, when it is the fruit of honest industry.
>
> She makes more than she and her household have occasion for; and therefore, when she has sufficiently stocked her family, *she sells fine linen and girdles to the merchants* (v. 24). Those families are likely to thrive that sell more than they buy...[9]

This exemplary woman has found a way to be productive from the base of her home, by meeting actual needs. She is not attempting to start a business selling crafts. Matthew Henry voiced caution about absorption in meaningless work that is scarcely one step away from doing nothing. The Proverbs 31 woman is not involved in that sort of busy work. No, she entrepreneurially involves herself in real estate ("She considers a field and buys it," v. 16), the farming business ("From her profits she plants a vineyard," v. 16) and a sewing enterprise, working with only the finest fabrics ("She makes linen garments and sells them, and supplies sashes for the merchants," v. 24). No, "she does not eat the bread of idleness" and as a result, "her own works praise her in the gates" (Proverbs 31:27, 31).

Entrepreneurial Brainstorming

Successful home businesses start from true needs. Think about it. What would you really like to have yourself, which is unavailable? What product? What service? If *you* sense the need for it, it is likely that others do, too. Meeting a genuine need better and less expensively than anyone else guarantees you have yourself a business. You don't *get* a job; you *make* one, as the documentary *The College Conspiracy* points out.

Here is a starter-list of all the things a young woman could do based out of her home:

- ❖ Bookkeeping
- ❖ Grow and sell produce
- ❖ Breed and sell animals
- ❖ Sew/clothing alterations
- ❖ Website design
- ❖ Graphic design
- ❖ Photography
- ❖ Personal Organization

(People love to hire women who are gifted in organization to come to their home and organize a cluttered room for them, and brainstorm filing systems, etc.)

❖ Laundry/ironing service
❖ Secretarial work for her father
❖ Sell things on eBay for others
   (Older people often have valuable items they would like to unload, and would sometimes be willing to pay a percentage to someone who knows how to sell on eBay.)
❖ Cook and deliver meals for a busy family
❖ Publish a cookbook that fits a unique market
❖ Tutor children
❖ Teach lessons (music, art, dance, sewing)
❖ Sell baked goods
   (Note: it is usually illegal to sell food that has not been cooked in an entirely stainless steel kitchen. However, some states have home food processing licenses. Other areas offer incubator kitchen programs where several entrepreneurs can bake in one commercial kitchen. Contact your local municipal planning office and search online to see what your state's guidelines are. However, think creatively. Perhaps a restaurant or local county fairgrounds would let you use their kitchen while they are closed.)

For ideas specific to your interests, review the questions in the vocational chapter, this time with the aim of turning your passion into a profitable home-based business.

Do things that you love to do, and do them publicly, where others can become aware of your ability. People look for those who are skilled in their work. You may land a job contract in this way, to work on as a stay-at-home daughter. One young lady who liked to edit books marked the typos in a book she was reading and sent them to the publisher. She ended up getting hired to edit more books for the publisher from home, all because she did what she loved, and did it publicly.

Getting Launched

So, what does a person need to do to get a business launched? Following are some tips that I have discovered in the process of launching my own entrepreneurial business.

Target Market

Identifying a specific demographic for your service or product may actually result in more customers than marketing to the world in general. Surprisingly, in most cases, the narrower a target market, the better the sales (assuming the business owner has a way to reach that market). This is because when the target market is clearly defined, by the time a product reaches the people within that market they will hardly have to think about purchasing, because the product or service meets their needs so directly.

So, consider: who is your target market? Busy mothers? Children? Engaged couples? The elderly? Messy people?

Once you have identified your target market, you can focus all your advertising on their unique interests. Think about where that type of people typically congregates. Then go there so that you can inform them of how your business can meet their needs. Once you're in their midst, hand out flyers and simply voice the fact that you are in business. Sending emails is another effective way of advertising to a group of people.

Have healthy marketing goals. An example of an unhealthy goal is "to get a response from each person I send a flyer to." It is impossible to control someone else's response, so a better goal would be to contact a certain number of people in a week.

Marketing becomes more effective when a business exists with the understanding of providing a solution to people's needs, rather than trying to *sell* someone something. Entrepreneurial businesses are really a way to serve people who do not have your time or expertise, but need the service that you offer.

Don't Go into Debt

Some think it is necessary to go into debt to start a business. However, borrowing money only adds stress to a new endeavor. Debt presumes on the future. It presumes the success of a venture. A much more stable way to start a business is to start small, and grow as revenue is earned. That way, if a better entrepreneurial idea surfaces, one can switch to it without worrying about having to pay off debt for a passé business.

Low Costs

Financial success is not all about high profit; a large degree of it comes from keeping expenses low. Low overhead costs mean it is possible to keep prices affordable enough that customers will buy. Business owners actually make more money in the long run when they offer affordable prices than when they make a high profit on each sale. This is because more people end up purchasing a product or service when it is inexpensive.

Take the classic filling station example, where a gas station undercuts another station across the street by a few pennies. Sure, they lose a few cents per gallon, but that loss is more than recouped by the additional number of customers who choose to buy gas there rather than across the street. Thus, low prices usually result in higher profit in the end.

Following are some tips for keeping your business expenses to a minimum in order to keep prices low for customers.

Practical Money-Saving Hints

Create a free website with www.weebly.com or a similar free web host (the URL will look like this: www.[yourbusiness].weebly.com). This way search engines will begin to help people find your products, and you have not spent any money for web development. At a future point, if it is evident that your business is profitable, you can register your own domain name without the word "weebly" in the web address.

If you have a mail order business, you can avoid having to run to the post office by printing shipping labels with postage online at usps.com. Better yet, if a customer paid through PayPal, just click on "print shipping label" when viewing the PayPal transaction, and you can do it all right there. Oftentimes shipping costs online are less expensive than in the post office itself.

Instead of buying boxes and mailing envelopes for mail orders, just begin saving every box and mailing envelope that comes to your house. You will be surprised how many you accumulate that are reusable, saving you the expense of buying packaging materials. This is also a helpful concept for packaging things to sell locally. Think of what you already have and use it.

Save Every Extra Penny

Many people think that because they have earned money, they have money to spend. Not so, if they want to get ahead in life.

An incredible amount of money can be lost in one year from little impulse purchases, like coffee. At four dollars twice a week, coffee purchases add up to $416 for the entire year.

Rather than allowing yourself to spend cash on trivial items, grow a vision of being able to purchase a home debt-free someday. (Or perhaps aim for another lofty goal such as traveling the world, investing in a musical instrument, or purchasing a car.) Whenever you are tempted to spend $20 impulsively, remind yourself that this same amount could, one day in the future, pay for the doorknob on the front door of your debt-free house. Such thinking makes it easier to save. Delayed gratification is not something you will regret when the time comes to reap the harvest of your discipline.

If you really want something, go home without buying it and wait overnight to see if you still want it by morning. Oftentimes, you will have found something you already have that works well in its stead, or you will have found a way to make it, borrow it, rent it, or buy it cheaper (perhaps used). If not, pray about it and tell the Heavenly Father about your desire and ask Him for it. Then wait. It is amazing how He provides what we ask of Him if it is His will for us to have it. As James said, "You do not have because you do not ask God..." (James 4:2 NIV).

With the money you save by making decisions like these, allow yourself to invest it wisely on better tools that will help you turn out your product more efficiently and more professionally. Tools (such as a better sewing machine, kitchen equipment, computer, etc.) are often a good place to invest money, because they usually retain their value and can be resold if need be. However, even in the purchase of these items, research thoroughly before buying them to find the best price possible online and to find any coupons that might be available. Search eBay, Craigslist, and Amazon. If the tool is not available there and you have to buy it new, search for price-reducing coupons through www.retailmenot.com.

Getting Legal

After seeing if your entrepreneurial business brings in income and is a satisfying endeavor, then it is a good idea to get the legal new-business paperwork out of the way. Every state is different, so go to www.[yourstate].gov (e.g. www.CA.gov) to find out for sure what you need to do to start a new business.

For a basic start-up business where you, individually, have the sole responsibility in the business, registering as a sole proprietorship (compared to an LLC or a corporation or partnership) will be simplest and least expensive.

Three primary legalities need to be taken care of:

1. Get a state Sales Tax License (except for the handful of states which do not charge sales tax). Sales Tax Licenses can be acquired through www.[yourstate].gov.

2. Obtain a business license from your local city hall. This is necessary if you live within the city limits. (In some areas, county and state business licenses are required as well—the city hall can inform you if that is the case.)

3. Optional: Register your business trade name with the Secretary of State (Google the term "Secretary of State [your state]" to find the correct website for your state). This keeps others from operating with your same business name, and also provides the necessary paperwork for opening a business bank account in order to take checks that are made out to your business name. However, there is no need to register if you are simply using your personal name

as the business name, which an author or photographer might do.

Tax Tips

Be sure to lay away 10% of your income for taxes at the end of the year if you expect to have income under $10,000 (20% if above $10,000). This will help you avoid the shock of not having that money on hand when income taxes come due.

> *How to Figure 10%*
>
> ~~~~~~~~~~~~~~~~~~~~~~~~~~~
>
> *Move decimal point one place to the left:*
>
> *$1,000.00 = $100.00*

You probably have heard of purchasing something as a "business expense," but do you know how that helps diminish taxes? Imagine that an entrepreneur named Elizabeth has a floral-arranging business, and in her first year she brings in $1,000. If she is in the 10% tax bracket, she pays $100 in taxes.

Every expense reduces the amount of income on which she gets taxed. If it costs Elizabeth $300 for flowers, and $200 in gas for deliveries, her total expense amount is basically subtracted from her gross income when she pays taxes, leaving $500 (all this is done behind the scenes, in the tax calculations).

> ### Ledger
> ~~~~~~~~~~~~~~~~~~~~~~~~
>
> $1,000 gross income
> −$300 flowers expense
> <u>−$200 gas expense</u>
> =$500 net profit

Her taxes are then calculated only from the remaining $500. So, she pays $50 in taxes, instead of the $100 she would have paid, had she not reported any expenses.

This is why it is helpful to keep track of business expenses. Receipts are important proof of each expense, so print out electronic confirmations of Web purchases and keep them and your physical receipts in storage for seven years, just in case the need arises to confirm an expense for the IRS.

Keep track of expenses such as shipping costs or the cost of raw materials or the price of equipment. Mileage can even be counted as a business expense if driving is a necessary part of a business—even for such local trips as driving to the post office or to deliver products. Keep track of miles in a little notebook kept in your car. Record the date, the beginning mileage number, and the ending mileage number when you have finished your errand. And also note the purpose of your trip (e.g. P.O., delivering,

Office Depot—purchasing supplies, etc.). At the end of the year, add up these miles and report them when figuring your income taxes.

Mileage Book				
Date:	To:	Beginning Mileage:	Ending Mileage:	Total Miles:
2/3/13	PO	63,880	63,900	20

Another idea for keeping income taxes to a minimum is to trade products for services or products your customer has that you need. Then, you do not receive any monetary/taxable income, and you obtain what you would have spent that money on anyway. Without having to pay taxes on it, trading allows your money to stretch further and have more buying power.

And while we are on the subject of taxes, don't forget to collect sales tax for local sales within your state and county or city. If a sale is made within your city, collect both state and city tax. If within your county, collect state and county tax. If the customer lives outside of both, but within your state, simply collect the state tax. If they live in another state, there is no need to collect any sales tax. Tax rates can be found online. You will have to pay these taxes at the end of the year whether or not your customers paid them, so it is important to collect taxes so you don't have to pay them out of your pocket.

Entrepreneurial Stewardship

After launching and legalizing a business, how does a Christian run one as a loyal steward of the Creator?

Gain... Save... Give... All You Can

John Wesley famously stated, "Gain [earn] all you can, Save all you can, Give all you can." This should be a Christian entrepreneur's practice.

Leveraging one's talents and turning them into a profitable business that meets other people's needs is the way to gain all you can. Wesley wrote in his sermonic essay, "The Use of Money":

> Gain all you can, by common sense, by using in your business all the understanding which God has given you. It is amazing to observe, how few do this; how men run on in the same dull track with their forefathers. You should be continually learning, from the experience of others, or from your own experience, reading, and reflection, to do everything you have to do better to-day than you did yesterday.[10]

Yet, he added three qualifications to the idea of gaining all you can. Gain all you can, but

1. Not at the expense of your health or life
2. Not by the hurt of your soul (through "conformity to some custom that is not consistent with a good conscience"[11])
3. Not to the disadvantage of a "neighbor" (leading people into vice through the sale of immoral material, etc.)

Any amount of gain in these areas is not worth it.

When Wesley said, "Save all you can," he did not encourage hoarding every spare penny, but rather, he emphasized frugality in spending—not spending any more than necessary. He wrote, "Do not throw [money] away in idle expenses, which is just the same as throwing it into the sea. Expend no part of it merely to gratify the desire of the flesh."[12]

Finally, he encouraged, "Give all you can." The reason to save (and also to stay out of debt, for that matter) is to be in a position to give. Wesley's life exemplified these three principles of his. In his most profitable year he made the equivalent of $1.4 million in today's money. But when he died, he had given so much away that he only left a few silver spoons behind. This is the blessed life—one in which it is possible to give rather than receive (see Acts 20:35).

The Creator has promised incredible blessings for those who give Him the firstfruits of their money in tithes. The prophet Malachi recorded this awesome promise of Yahweh:

> "Bring all the tithes into the storehouse, that there may be food in My house, and try Me now in this," says the Lord of hosts, "If I will not open for you the windows of heaven and pour out for you such blessing that there will not be room enough to receive it. And I will rebuke the devourer for your sakes, so that he will not destroy the fruit of your ground, nor shall the vine fail to bear fruit for you in the field." (Malachi 3:10-11)

Who wouldn't want to give into that kind of system? The idea is: You give God the first 10% of your money, and He will bless and protect you.

God declares, "those who honor Me I will honor" (1 Samuel 2:30). How eager we should be to give of our money for His purposes once we recognize that we are really stewards of *His* money. The more productive our entrepreneurial businesses, the more we can give.

Work Heartily

Although it is the entrepreneur's joy to be able to do work she loves, remember that work is *work*, and will not always be pleasant. Every job has its tedious moments. Sometimes it is even necessary to do work in a field that is not one's preference for a while.

Financial Freedom counselor and author Dave Ramsey suggests making it a habit to do the things no one wants to do—such as emptying the trash. You will become indispensable, and people will see your work ethic and often find work for you, as Ramsey reveals in this story from his book, *EntreLeadership*:

> You never know who is watching. As a teenager I went with my family to a wonderful steak house for dinner. Our waitress, who was probably not working in her life's calling, was on fire. She was there at the table taking the order and bringing the food with a smile and an energy that every restaurant manager dreams of. My dad hired her the next week to sell real estate for our family real estate company. The first year, this twenty-something young lady sold a million dollars' worth of

real estate, which in today's dollars would be about ten million. You never know who is watching when you are working for money, so do it with excellence."[13]

So, as the Word of God commands, "Whatever you do, do it heartily, as to the Lord and not to men, knowing that from the Lord you will receive the reward of the inheritance; for you serve the Lord Christ" (Colossians 3:23). So, whether working on one's own brainchild venture or simply a duty-bound responsibility, working joyfully and with initiative will bring advancement in life.

Entrepreneurship Second to Family

Running a home business can be all-consuming. As the joke goes, entrepreneurs only work half time—12 hours a day! For a woman, entrepreneurship brings the temptation to work on improving and operating her business at the expense of her family. After all, customers always take first priority. Or should they? Someone wisely observed, "When juggling a home and a business, it is almost always the home ball that drops, hardly ever the business." So we must be on guard against this usurpation.

The Proverbs 31 woman did not work at her home business to the exclusion of tending to her own household. As the writer tells, "She looks well to the ways of her household" (Proverbs 31:27 NASB). Doing that should be first priority.

Successful though an entrepreneurial business could be, the important thing is to invest time and energy in it *after* blessing our families. Cooking a healthy dinner needs to be a higher priority than building a website, for instance.

How much happier the home environment will be when the needs of those closest to us are met first.

Better Than College

The number one training ground for CEOs of S&P 500 companies was not college, but the "school of hard knocks" (life), as a 2010 Bloomberg study revealed.[14] If it worked for them, it can work for you. After graduating from college, many people drool to own their own business, so why not jump straight to entrepreneurship without the college interlude?

Even without winning the $100,000 Thiel Fellowship, starting one or several businesses puts youth ahead of peers who sink deeper and deeper into school debt. No classroom business education matches the education that comes from actually running a business. *Needing* to learn accounting, management, and marketing skills will make concepts stick far better than a hypothetical classroom example. When it is your own business, you will want to find the best way of doing things, and to do that you will eagerly study books written by experts who have discovered and shared optimum business practices.

Ultimately, after doing our best to develop the finest product, to control expenses, and to market effectively, it is the Almighty Who sends the increase (see Deuteronomy 8:18). We are helpless without His blessing. Therefore, it is a beautiful thing to pray at the end of the day, "establish the work of our hands for us" (Psalm 90:17). He loves to do just that for His faithful stewards.

Success Without College Testimony:
$40,000 a year in LEGO Sales

"I decided not to go to college for several reasons: the time commitment, the high costs, and my desire to stay out of every form of debt. Since learning is part of real-life, everyday events, I was not interested in paying to take classes about what I could learn with hands-on experience. This way I could also make and save money while learning, instead of spending it!

So at the age of nineteen, I started off on this plan. I had just received a small inheritance from my grandfather. With $2,000 of that money and a very small amount of my savings, I began selling LEGO toys on eBay. When I made a sale, I would re-invest in more merchandise, gradually increasing the net worth of my business. I eventually purchased my own domain, adeal4u.net, where I have a whole store of LEGO. Over the first five years, with much diligence and hard work, I was able to increase those original dollars to over $100,000 in inventory and other assets. This was accomplished even while taking off three to five months per year for traveling and other activities.

My business now has the potential of making $40,000 or more per year if I work full time. One of the best aspects of running my own business is that I get to choose when and how much I work. I am very happy with the decision I made to skip college."

—JONATHAN WILLIAMS (25), fulfilled business owner

10

THE MRS DEGREE

"Let each woman have her own husband"
(1 Corinthians 7:2)

" 'It is not good for the man to be alone; I will make him a
helper suitable for him.' " (Genesis 2:18 NASB)

"Rather than a ball and chain that weighs us down," states Glenn Stanton in his book, *The Ring Makes All the Difference*, marriage "consistently lifts our physical and physiological health, keeps us away from doctors, speeds our recoveries from illness, and boosts our contentment."[1] Those statements are not just wishful exaggerations about the benefits of marriage; they are facts confirmed by much scientific research. No wonder so many young ladies inwardly long to obtain a MRS (Marriage is Really Swell!) degree above any other.

Radical Feminist Robbery

Though marriage is a well-founded desire inherent in most girls before they go to college, radical feminism has deeply penetrated university campuses and brainwashed girl after girl into thinking that a woman who marries and gives birth to children tragically wastes her potential. Feminist ideology portrays traditional marriage as a drag. One influential feminist, Germaine Greer, wrote, "If women are to effect a significant amelioration [making something unsatisfactory better] in their condition it seems obvious that they must refuse to marry."[2] She also stated, "The plight of mothers is more desperate than that of other women, and the more numerous the children the more hopeless the situation seems to be."[3] In other words, marrying and having a family restricts a woman from experiencing a fulfilling career.

Colleges publicize the idea that "no woman should have to deny herself any opportunities because of her special responsibilities to her children."[4] And so, many young ladies have bought the lie that pursuing a career is of far higher importance than investing in wifedhood and motherhood.

However, as they grow old, these women who have generated this deception now find that no children or grandchildren exist to make their elderly years sparkle, and no love-of-their-life sits by their side to provide companionship on a porch swing at the end of the day. Feminists have what they thought they wanted—career independence—but what they did not account for is the price tag of their stridency—hollow loneliness. For many it is too late to go back and embrace God's blessed design of family. Their biology will not permit it.

The selfsame Germaine Greer as quoted above shocked the world by stating in May 2000, at the age of sixty-one, that she inwardly longed to be a mother after all. A headline in the premier issue of *Aura* magazine shouted her heart's uncovered secret: "I WAS DESPERATE FOR A BABY AND I HAVE THE MEDICAL BILLS TO PROVE IT." She continued to confess, "I still have pregnancy dreams, waiting with vast joy and confidence for something that will never happen." As analyst Charles Krauthammer commented about this revelation:

> The one adjective rarely attached to Greer was domestic. And now she reveals the hollowness that haunts her, the terrible sorrow she feels at what she lost: her chance for motherhood. ... A joy [feminists] deliberately gave up, under the terms of the original feminist contract, in the name of autonomy and advancement.[5]

Feminist leader Simone de Beauvoir stated in a 1974 issue of *The Saturday Review*, "No woman should be authorized to stay at home and raise her children. Society should be totally different. Women should not have that choice, precisely because if there is such a choice, too many women will make that one." Deep down, even feminists know that women were created to be mothers. Their propaganda about what constitutes true fulfillment is a big lie and it is not broadcasted for the benefit of women after all.*

---

* To read about how the state and socialist ideology are those who actually benefit from feminism, read ...

College Testimony: Onslaught of Feminism

"I attended a small Christian college; nevertheless, I encountered humanism and feminism in many of my classes. Instead of fighting the onslaught of novel interpretations and clever feminist hermeneutics, I took copious notes and diligently worked for the coveted *A* in every class. I thought I was finally becoming sophisticated and erudite. A steady undercurrent flowed through every class and seasoned conversations with peers: 'You're on your own now; time to grow up and be your own person.' My freshman orientation class focused upon cutting home ties. With each passing day, my family sank into the distant past, and I saw myself as an individual, my future unconnected with anyone else.

This individualistic shift in my foundation paved the way for everything to follow. The early protests I'd felt against feminism and humanism in the classroom softened. As each semester passed, I objected less and less. Over time, like Chinese water torture, the bitter words began to seep through my psyche. Doubts planted as tiny seeds grew into monstrous weeds, filling me with apprehension.

At this point I decided marriage wasn't for me. All my dreams of marrying and having lots of children were silly, I thought. Hadn't I just invested in four

... *Passionate Housewives Desperate for God* by Jennie Chancey and Stacy McDonald, and *So Much More* by Anna Sofia Botkin and Elizabeth Botkin.

years of 'higher' education? Why should I waste all my talents and gifts on being 'just' a homemaker? So I hardened my heart and congratulated myself on my individualism. College turned me into a full-fledged Christian feminist.

But God wasn't finished with me, and I've never stopped thanking Him for that. He began bringing people into my life who gently tugged at the blinders I had put on in college. I saw husbands and wives who deeply loved each other and had vibrant ministries through their homes.

So, I eventually disowned feminism and repented to my parents, and six months later God brought into my life the man I would marry. Sixteen years later, we are the blessed parents of ten children. There are times I look around and catch my breath, thinking of all the wonderful lives that wouldn't be here if I'd embraced my barren 'empowerment' and rejected biblical family life. The lure may be sweet, but the trap is bitter. I lament the years I wasted in college."

—JENNIE CHANCEY, third-generation home educator, author, encourager of young women wholeheartedly embracing the role God has graciously designed for them, founder of www.beautifulwomanhood.org

Perhaps the Creator *did* know what He was doing when He designed women primarily to be nurturing homemakers rather than driven career women. If the very leaders of the feminist movement are themselves secretly feeling unfulfilled without a family, why should we follow their unproven advice to value a career as a woman's best ultimate aim?

G. K. Chesterton had a high regard for the position of a woman within her home. He wrote:

> To be Queen Elizabeth within a definite area, deciding sales, banquets, labours, and holidays; to be Whitely within a certain area, providing toys, boots, cakes and books; to be Aristotle within a certain area, teaching morals, manners, theology, and hygiene; I can imagine how this can exhaust the mind, but I cannot imagine how it could narrow it. How can it be a large career to tell other people about the Rule of Three, and a small career to tell one's own children about the universe? How can it be broad to be the same thing to everyone and narrow to be everything to someone? No, a woman's function is laborious, but because it is gigantic, not because it is minute.

So, it is just fine to desire a MRS degree more than a college degree. In fact, not only is the desire to be married legitimate, but it is also biblical and noble.

How Will "He" Find Me?

"But how," you might ask, "does a girl obtain a MRS degree without the aid of a university campus where marriageable young folks congregate?" For the young women who mingle in a college social setting in hopes of finding their matches, the primary type of guy there is not usually the kind of man who a believer would want to marry. It is true that some ladies have found godly husbands through college, but this is becoming an exception to the rule, due to the type of life that college settings foster.

Where Are the Christian Men?

At the supposedly Christian college I attended, I knew about a dozen Christian girls but I could only name two nominal Christian young men on the entire campus. One was a new Japanese Christian who was just learning how to pray (he was stuck in a class about homosexuality and was starving for discipleship); and the other was a pastor's son who chased every girl in sight and mocked her biblical convictions! There is something wrong when there are basically no Christian men on a Christian college campus.

Many young men in college are guys who refuse to grow up. Granted, not all of them, but many or most are primarily interested in playing their days away through video games and undisciplined living. If they show interest in a young woman, they usually do so in order to get the "milk without the cow," as the saying goes. Preparing to provide for a family and commit to a wife for life are not typically two goals of a college-going young man. Hoping to find a godly husband in such an environment is an unrealistic prospect.

How much better to intentionally plant oneself in social environments where most of the young men have qualities to be desired in a future husband, rather than where most do not? Marriage is a lifetime commitment, so it is extremely important to consciously choose one's companions among those who could be quality marriage potential rather than to subconsciously become more and more attached to charming (though ungodly) young men who are in great supply at most colleges.

In college, it is easy to lose track of the importance of long-term character and godliness in a guy after having spent years studying, eating, and recreating with him. Within the artificial living environment of a university, he is unproven, and as a young woman it is easy to be blind to his faults, due to considering him as more of a companion than a life partner (even if that is where the relationship might be headed). Conversely, in real-life settings, where a young woman chooses what type of young men to be around, she can stay more alert to character flaws than if she has been buddy-buddy with the guy daily for years. Seeing him interact with his family reveals his true character.

Even in cases where a godly couple miraculously does meet at college, they usually delay getting married in order to focus on graduating. In addition to increasing the couple's sexual temptation with each other, this also potentially diminishes the size of their family. The loss of time to obey the Creator's very first command, "be fruitful and multiply," has eternal impact on the number of people who will populate heaven.

Not only does college often sap away valuable child-bearing years, but also if a young woman falls in love with a *non*believer at college and marries him, their children's faith will hang in the balance. Considering potential children might seem irrelevant when making a college decision, but think of it! What are souls worth?

Let's not limit God. It is possible for the Almighty to cause *him* to find *you* outside of college. Being open to the Heavenly Father's matchmaking and His timing, instead of insisting upon it conforming to our college goals, could result in a blessed outcome.

Pining for Marriage

Some young women who choose not to go to college tend to pine away for marriage instead. Because they value a family more than a career, when marriage does not arrive right away they do not know what to do with themselves. When this dissatisfaction strikes, it is often very helpful to ask: *Would getting married really solve my discontentment right now?*

To reach the answer to this question, specifically state what it is that is currently making you discontent. Sometimes you may be surprised to find that it is not really because you are single that you are discontent, but because you do not feel well, or are having relational difficulties with those around you and want to escape them, or you lack big enough goals to pursue in the meantime before marriage.

Once you have pinpointed exactly what is causing you to feel discontent, then you can ask yourself, would marriage really fix this? If a young lady is fighting the flu for a long time, getting married tomorrow will not eliminate the flu. Or, if marriage is the only goal on her horizon, what happens once she is married and her husband is at work all day? She will likely still be discontent. Or perhaps she thinks, "If I could just get married I wouldn't have to deal with relating to this family member anymore. Their idiosyncrasies really bother me, so I want to just get married." But, wait! After marriage, that person still exists. They remain related to her, so she will still have to figure out how to lovingly relate to them.

Once you have identified the problem and realize you cannot escape it through marriage, you can embrace the challenge of improving the bothersome situation, instead of being frustrated about not being able to achieve your hope of getting married. For example, if a girl is not happy with her personal health, she can work toward improving it through achieving specific goals (such as exercising or eating better, etc.). Or if she is discontent with a family relationship, she can compel herself to draw nearer to that person (rather than farther away), and figure out how to become more understanding towards him or her.

Ultimately, discontentment surges within us because we are longing for the Messiah's kingdom to come. Experiencing the alienating results of the Fall causes us to long for restoration to un-fallen paradise. We're discontent with our own sin nature. We're longing to move on, out of this fallen state. We think the answer is marriage. The truth is, we are ultimately yearning to be united with our heavenly Bridegroom. That is the only marriage into which we can move away from our sin nature. *That* marriage will satisfy every longing. Realizing that earthly marriage to a fallen human is only a God-given *taste* of what is to come helps us not to feel so discontent while waiting. It helps to know that even after marriage, we will still be waiting. This thought also keeps us from loading the idea of marriage with unrealistic expectations. Yes, there will still be things to disappoint us even when "the one" arrives, and understanding this will help our expectations have less far to crash.

Marriage is definitely a state to be desired, but Paul has encouraged us to be content in *whatever* state we find ourselves (Philippians 4:11). The only reason to be discontent or despondent about any situation is if the only world we are living for is this one. Greater things are yet to come!

It's a Real Longing

Sometimes the longing for a soul mate is very strong and it is not a discontentment with other circumstances, but a real longing for *him*. Longing for marriage is not wrong. Sometimes God instills a desire in us in order to fulfill it. If the Lord has put in us the desire to be restored to the side of man from where we were taken (as Eve was from her Adam) then it might not be right to subdue that longing in an effort to be content.

In Adam's case, God made him painfully conscious of his need for a mate. The story progressed this way: God *planned* to give Adam a helpmeet (Genesis 2:18); God caused Adam to *feel his need* for a wife, in the process of naming the animals, and seeing that they each had a mate but he did not (2:19-20); and then God *fulfilled* the desire by creating Eve as Adam's wife (2:21-22). For Adam to have said, "Well, I'd like a wife, but I'm going to learn to be content without one" was not God's plan. He wanted Adam to keenly feel his need for a helpmeet so he would be truly grateful for God's gift when she arrived.

Desiring marriage is a wholesome yearning, one that God created and sometimes allows to burn unquenched for a while for purposes only He knows. However, to impatiently want to be married now (before God's timing) is to ignore the purpose God has given to each of us before marriage. Perhaps we do not have to feel completely satisfied with singleness, but we should definitely become fulfilled while single. Adam was given responsibility before he was given a wife to help him accomplish it. His single life had purpose as he fulfilled his assignment to name the animals and take dominion over all of creation. Getting married only allowed him to be more productive at what he was already doing.

Adam did not wait to start living until he had a wife, and neither should we. Life is what happens while we're waiting for life to start. Marriage came to women in the Bible while they were productively busy rather than lazily pining for it. Ruth was working in the fields, Rachel was shepherding her father's sheep, Abigail was serving food to an army of men, and Rebecca was watering camels when her marriage opportunity arrived. God has a purpose for our time now, and we please Him by heartily throwing ourselves into the responsibilities in front of each of us.

Therefore, the lack of a college goal should not signify the lack of all goals except marriage. A life worth living contains goals, rather than a void that comes from chucking college in order to sit on the couch waiting for a lover to swoop down and carry one away. As Glenn Stanton pointed out in *The Ring Makes All the Difference*, marital "happiness is never a destination we can run straight toward. ... The happiest people are typically busy doing other things."[6]

Occupy Till He Comes

Until we have homes under our own jurisdiction, we can serve in our current homes. As authors Anna Sofia and Elizabeth Botkin say, "the cookies you bake today are no less valuable than the cookies you will bake tomorrow!" Let us be encouraged by knowing that blessing the family around us today through domestic finesse—loving being at home and showing it through excellence—is just as glorious as puttering about in our own homes someday will be.

How can you best occupy till your man comes (see Luke 19:13)? Prepare for what you hope for. If you want to be a homemaker someday, learn now so when the time comes you will be capable and confident at the skill of running a home. There are many other ways to occupy till he comes. Launch a successful home business. Go ahead ... do it! Begin a thought-out plan for sharpening your mental acuity through reading top-notch books, taking courses, and apprenticing. Set goals in all sorts of subjects and include specific steps for reaching them. Finally, serve, serve, serve with the mindset of: What would the Messiah do if He were in this situation? When entering a room, switch from thinking: *Here I am; will you like me?* to: *There you are; how can I serve you?* A fulfilled life brings the greatest happiness—whether or not it is accompanied by a MRS degree.

In the meantime, the following quote from Louisa May Alcott's beloved *Little Women* offers some inspiration on living life cheerfully while single:

> Jo had got so far, she was learning to do her duty, and to feel unhappy if she did not, but to do it cheerfully, ah, that was another thing! She had often said she wanted to do something splendid, no matter how hard, and now she had her wish, for what could be more beautiful than to devote her life to Father and Mother, trying to make home as happy to them as they had to her? And if difficulties were necessary to increase the splendor of the effort, what could be harder for a restless, ambitious girl than to give up her own hopes, plans, and desires, and cheerfully live for others? Providence had taken her at her word. Here was the task, not what she had expected, but better because self had no part in it. Now, could she do it? She decided that she would try.[7]

As you wait to see if God's plan for you involves marriage, be assured that "he who finds a wife finds a good thing, and obtains favor from the Lord" (Proverbs 18:22); and it is an equally good matter to be the one who is *found* by a husband.

If we are obedient to His will for us—going places or staying home, being active or being still, as He leads—He can bring a husband to each of us for whom He destines marriage. After all, He brought Adam a mate, even when there were no other people in existence. Talk about the odds being against finding someone to marry! The same God who made that match is still God today, and He doesn't need college to accomplish His purposes. An undergraduate degree is not required in order to obtain a Masters in Relational Self-Sacrifice (MRS degree).

No-Degree Testimony: College Does Not Equip a Girl for Marriage and Motherhood

"During my teenage years, I wanted to do lots of things. Sometimes what I wanted to do involved going to college, other times, just shorter classes to get certifications in this or that. As I got older, I realized that I really wanted to be a stay-at-home wife and mother. I knew that was God's calling on my life, and I had been taught all my growing-up years that there was no higher calling for a woman. Though I pursued different jobs in the meantime to keep me occupied and pay some of my expenses, I never wanted to go to college after I got older. I realize, now that I am married, that college would have been a complete waste of time and money for me.

For one thing, there is nothing that they teach you there that you can't learn on your own if you have the discipline and ambition. A young woman can further her education without spending thousands of dollars and countless hours in a den of iniquity to do it. Also, there are plenty of jobs, both inside the home and out, that a girl doesn't need a degree for in order to excel.

If a young woman is trying to live a Godly life, and subsequently to attract a Godly young man, there are far more important things to invest time in than college. College life generally doesn't move people closer to God and their family, or teach them how to raise children or run a household. Many more practical lessons could be learned doing tasks such as childcare, serving others, or just keeping and excelling at even a simple job where you learn to relate to those in authority and the public. Strictly from a practical sense, if a young woman truly desires to have a good marriage and a happy home, college isn't the place to learn how to do that."

—BRITNEY WILLIAMS, happily married
(to Jay, p. 154), mother of two

11

SURVEYING SUCCESS

"He holds success in store for the upright."
(Proverbs 2:7 NIV)

What is success? The world says success comes from having a college degree, an absorbing career, a large house, and no more than one or two children. Never mind the debt, the unfulfillment, and the depression that too often accompanies this version of success.

Perhaps we ought to look to the One who created us to define the standard of success for which we should aim. So, what does the Bible say constitutes success? As mentioned earlier, the godly person of Psalm 1 "does not walk in the counsel of the wicked, nor stand in the way of sinners, nor sit in the seat of scoffers." As a result of not participating in these college-like activities, "he shall be like a tree planted by the rivers of water, that brings forth its fruit in its season, whose leaf also shall not wither; and whatever he does shall prosper" (Psalm 1:3). Prospering in all ways, not just monetarily, is the ultimate form of success. Therefore, leaving the counsel of the wicked, the way of sinners, and the seat of scoffers is the first step to success.

In God's view, success results from obedience to His commands. Obedience is the place of blessing, and being blessed is God's definition of successfulness. Nowhere is this stated in a more heart-warming way than in Deuteronomy 28:1-13:

> Now it shall come to pass, if you diligently obey the voice of the Lord your God, to observe carefully all His commandments which I command you today, ... all these blessings shall come upon you and overtake you ... Blessed shall you be in the city, and blessed shall you be in the country. Blessed shall be the fruit of your body, the produce of your ground and the increase of your herds, the increase of your cattle and the offspring of your flocks. Blessed shall be your basket and your kneading bowl. Blessed shall you be when you come in, and blessed shall you be when you go out.
>
> The Lord will cause your enemies who rise against you to be defeated before your face; they shall come out against you one way and flee before you seven ways. The Lord will command the blessing on you in your storehouses and in all to which you set your hand, and He will bless you in the land which the Lord your God is giving you. ... And the Lord will grant you plenty of goods, in the fruit of your body, in the increase of your livestock, and in the produce of your ground, in the land of which the Lord swore to your fathers to give you.

The Lord will open to you His good treasure, the heavens, to give the rain to your land in its season, and to bless all the work of your hand. You shall lend to many nations, but you shall not borrow. And the Lord will make you the head and not the tail; you shall be above only, and not be beneath, if you heed the commandments of the Lord your God, which I command you today, and are careful to observe them.

What a passage! God speaks of success in every area of life for those who obey. The world's definition pales in comparison—its narrow view of success only involves a race for filthy lucre. Striving to obtain the blessing of the Creator should be of far higher value to us than seeking the worldly-minded accolade of success.

A person could have a million dollars in the bank and live in a movie-star mansion, but be miserable because of living a life of disobedience to the principles of the Scripture. The world would call him successful, but God would not. He says in Psalm 1 that the man is successful who does not find companions among the wicked (at college?), and who meditates on His laws in order to obey them. It ought to be our greatest desire to study the Scriptures in order to discover what more we can obey to bring joy to our Creator and blessings to ourselves. When Joshua took Moses' place as leader of Israel, he gave them this similar charge for how to be successful:

This Book of the Law shall not depart from your mouth, but you shall meditate in it day and night, that you may observe to do according to all that is written in it. For then you will make your way prosperous, and *then you will have good success*. (Joshua 1:8, emphasis added)

This different understanding of success is part of the dichotomy between those who think not going to college will result in failure and those who know not obeying the Lord's principles will result in ultimate failure. The two discuss success on completely different levels and think the other is being irrational, when really they each have a different standard by which they measure success.

The bottom line to decide before the Creator is, as Randy Alcorn put it, "Am I living to hear others say of me, 'He's a great success!'—or to have You say to me, 'Well done, My good and faithful servant'?"[1] Obedience is the place of blessing, but the world may not recognize that blessing as success. The Bible called Joseph a successful man while he was a slave in an Egyptian household (see Genesis 39:2). Slavery and having one's brothers turn antagonistic is not exactly most people's perception of success. But because he kept himself from evil, the Lord was with Joseph, which equals the best success a believer could hope to have.

As Doug Phillips points out in his Entrepreneurial Bootcamp audio series, a person might fail at business and yet be a success in God's eyes by being obedient. Perhaps an issue of obedience might be the very point over which a person loses material gain. It is true that fruitfulness is God's reward for obeying, but how it manifests depends on God's will. Therefore, success is not measurable by income or status.

A Mother's Testimony: Success Differs

" What is success? Twenty years ago, this thought-provoking question asked by my young son prompted me to think. Peering into his inquisitive eyes, I realized God had designed his life for a purpose. It became clear: For each of my six children, success is accomplishing the purpose for which they have been designed.

This led me to another question: Is college always necessary for success? Certain risks concerned me. While immersed in the college culture, my child would need the spiritual strength to swim upstream through worldly philosophies, traps, and lifestyles. After college, most likely he or she would risk drowning in a sea of debt. For young women, the debt issue is especially alarming. An obligation to repay college loans interferes with a mother's natural desire and freedom to create a nurturing home.

I concluded: If my child's purpose could be accomplished without college, we would ask God to direct us to His alternative paths of preparation. And He did—He led several of our children to go to trade schools instead of college. The most protected and providentially productive path is always the one God chooses!"

—LYNNE GULLO, wife and mother of six,
author of *Markers* Western civilization curriculum

In Ecclesiastes 10:10, the wisest man in the world said, "wisdom brings success." Thus, if our true reason for desiring higher education is to achieve success, we must wrestle with the question, "Is it wise to go to college?" The path of wisdom brings lasting success. If we conclude that college is a place of immorality and indoctrination rather than wisdom, then perhaps college does not offer the best route to success.

Throughout this book, we have seen many examples of avenues to success that *are* wise, pure, and blessed by the Lord. Knowing the sobering statistics that are the result of colleges' attack on students' faith, fidelity, and finances, you too may choose to chuck college for something better.

"You will show me the path of life;
In Your presence is fullness of joy;
At Your right hand are pleasures forevermore."
(Psalm 16:11)

An Encouraging Letter…

Dear College-Omitting Youth,

"So [Israel] came up to Baal-perazim, and David smote [the Philistines] there. Then David said, God has broken my enemies by my hand, like the bursting forth of waters. Therefore they called the name of that place Baal-perazim [Lord of breaking through]." (1 Chronicles 14:11)

Notice how David likened God's power to the bursting forth of waters (a flood, really) in this verse.

He was saying that when the God of the breakthrough shows up and releases His power, it will be like a flood of His goodness, a flood of His favor, a flood of healing, a flood of new opportunity.

Think about how powerful water is. Three or four inches of water can pick up a huge car that weighs thousands of pounds and move it all around. Look at how whole houses have floated in several of the major floods this world has experienced in the past few years. Nothing can stop the force of that water! Anything that is in its way is moved!

You may have difficulties that look extremely large, obstacles that look impassable, dreams that look unobtainable. But know this: when the God of the breakthrough releases a flood of His power, nothing can stop it. You need to get ready, not for a trickle, not for a stream, not for a river, but for a flood of God's favor, a tidal wave of His goodness, a tsunami of His increase! Dare to believe that God is going to overwhelm you with victory in every area of your life as you seek His face and step out in faith to do His will!

Blessings,
Mrs. Lauren Heath

APPENDIX A

NO REGRETS!

EXTENDED TESTIMONY OF A YOUNG LADY'S SUCCESS WITHOUT COLLEGE

"I run in the path of Your commands, for You have set my heart free." (Psalm 119:32 NIV)

Hi. My name is Megan Miller. After finishing home school high school, I chose to take a different route with my life than what our culture says is "normal." I chose to not go to college, but instead, to stay at home; to increase in knowledge and prepare for my future in a different way. Even though I knew that I didn't want to do the "normal college thing," as I moved through my last couple years of high school and then graduated, I still had a hard time with being "different" than the majority of my friends who were all making significant decisions about college and their future lives. It felt like they were doing big, important things. Even though I was convinced that I was choosing what God had shown me for my future, it was hard on me to be misunderstood by adult friends, who reacted to my choice with comments that made me feel as though they disapproved, as if what I had chosen to do was very insignificant or a waste of time and talent. But as time went on, I was able to gain more perspective. I was able to see my life and choices compared with others, and I have been, and continue to be, very grateful for the way that the Lord led me.

I spent several years playing in a college orchestra, and taking music lessons from teachers at the college. So even though I was not an official college student (you could say that I was in the college, but not of it), I still had the opportunity to observe college life. These are some of the things I saw...

Problems with College

Debt: This was a major reason why I chose to not go to a college. I believe in a very literal understanding of Romans 13:8, "Owe nothing to anyone except to love one another..." (NASB) The amount of debt that is accumulated during the college years creates a bondage that holds a person back from being able to more forward in freedom into whatever God has for him/her. The expenses of college life are enormous. (There are better options, if someone does want a degree. One of my brothers tested out of two years of college by CLEP testing, and earned an Associate degree, and only spent $1,500, including textbooks and graduation fees.)

Waste of Time: Studying and learning are good things. However, colleges have degree requirements that take up long periods of time. They require many classes that have nothing to do with the student's field of study. As a result, what should take a short time, takes a very long time. Therefore, time and money are wasted.

Pressure to Fit in: It's hard to stand alone for a belief or principle, especially if one surrounds oneself with a culture that is opposed to one's beliefs. This is even true in Christian colleges where the classes *might* be based on scriptural things, but the culture is still an environment that is removed from real life, and very much peer-influenced.

Issue of Authority: If a young woman attends a college, she has voluntarily placed herself under the authority of the administration and the professors. Perhaps she could stand up for her beliefs if differences arise, but she has given them the authority to affect her grade and degree, which equals giving them authority to affect her future.

Question of Fulfillment: According to the general opinions that I heard, which were "proven" by the photographs in the advertisements sent out by colleges, going to college is supposed to provide great levels of fulfillment. Everyone looks so satisfied and happy. The idea communicated is, "This will prepare you for your exciting future!" "This degree will equip you so that you can get a really good job." "This will provide security." "This degree that you will get proves to everyone that you are smart and important."

Unfortunately, as I have observed many people, I have seen something very different than what those pictures portray. Going to college doesn't give the sense of identity that each person is looking for. It does not provide any kind of lasting fulfillment. It does not provide security. Many of my friends have struggled as they finished a degree, graduated, and then realized that they still need something else to take them where they were hoping to be. A degree is often like a mirage in the desert.

After Graduating High School

My choice to not go to college did not have anything to do with an aversion to study or learning. It was not as if I finished high school, shut my last book, and said, "Whew! I hope I never see a textbook again!" On the contrary, I looked forward to learning and studying subjects that were not a normal part of high school. I was excited to have the time to read, and grow in skills. There was so much I wanted to learn!

When life is not strictly scheduled, it is easy to waste time. As I moved into the years after graduation, I knew that it was important, vital even, to fill my time with projects or plans of great and/or eternal value. (This doesn't necessarily mean big, dramatic, or impressive activities ... most of life is not filled with impressive things ... but simply worthy activities.) I knew that I needed vision and purpose, otherwise I would get bored and lose my perspective and priorities or I would fritter away months or years of my life ... time for which I will be held accountable by God. I didn't want to be like the man in the parable of the talents (Matthew 25:14-30) who took what he had been given and simply buried it.

I had several friends who didn't want to go to college. They had short-term ideas at the beginning, such as, "I'm looking forward to doing some sewing." or, "I think that I'm going to help a farrier for a while." but before long, those things held no interest, and gave them no help toward moving forward in life. Often there were expectations about how soon after high school they would get married, and when that didn't happen as soon as had been hoped, it brought a vacuum of purpose, a feeling of "what am I supposed to do now?"

(Note to parents: often this "vacuum of purpose" is largely the fault of the parents who have not prepared their children for the years after high school. You have the great opportunity to shape your children's thinking and their vision for the coming years. Prepare them to seek the Lord's will, prepare them to serve others and help them to find ways of doing that, prepare them to continue learning and increasing their skills after high school, and prepare them (especially the girls) to live useful, productive, fulfilling lives in between the years of graduation and marriage.)

Opportunities

In choosing to not go to college, I had worlds of opportunity open to me. I had liberty to step into whatever the Lord brought. I experienced fulfillment and joy in what He gave me to do.

I had already begun a private music studio, teaching violin and piano, when I was fourteen. After graduating, I had time to expand it. I usually had anywhere from fifteen to thirty students a week. I have never felt a lack, or an inadequacy from not having a degree. Teaching music was an ideal job for me. It provided adequately for my financial needs. (I made more money per hour than any of my friends working "regular" jobs.) I had the flexibility to cancel or reschedule lessons if needed. And, something that I valued very highly was that I had daily opportunities to speak into people's lives. I could minister to them, and help to shape their lives. To me, it was far more than just teaching someone how to play violin or piano. I found it very fulfilling (and still do).

Another benefit in not going to college was a freedom of time and resources. When the Lord opened the door for me to go to Israel several times, I had no time commitments or debt hindering me from moving forward. The freedom to do that opened more doors as I traveled and met people. I've been able to learn, minister and serve, travel and experience because of that freedom.

In choosing to stay home, I had the time to be a 4-H leader and superintendent. I was able to invest into the lives of "my" kids and their parents, helping them to learn valuable skills and knowledge. I loved my years of being a 4-H leader, and I appreciate so much being able to see the friendships that developed and continue, and the result of many seeds planted, of truths shared, and of skills learned.

My sister and I also took time in those "college years" to lead a girls' Bible study. Again, I so valued the opportunity to serve and minister, to plant seeds of truth, to invest into the lives of those girls. My sister and I learned and grew as much as they did.

I had the freedom to be very active in my congregation as a worship dance teacher. Again, as I taught others, and as part of the praise team, I was also learning valuable skills myself that the Lord has used over the years, opening up more doors of opportunity.

Because my parents taught my siblings and me to work hard and to enjoy serving others, we have never lacked for job opportunities. We have always been in high demand, and have often had to turn down job offers because we were so busy. Never have our futures been hindered, and never have work opportunities been lacking because we didn't have college degrees.

Probably the most valuable result of not going to college was that it gave me the opportunity to serve my family and to maintain my relationships with my parents, brothers, and sister. I chose to stay under my parents' authority and remain in that place of blessing. That statement may sound like it would be said in a soft whispery tone with a sappy little smile by a girl who never left her house, never had her own thoughts, and never had plans to do anything with her own life. But change the picture in your mind because deliberately choosing to place yourself under authority requires great strength. When you're a kid, it is one thing to be under your parents' authority. When you're an adult, it's something completely different.

Choosing to actively serve your family is probably one of the most unglamorous ministries there is. (Probably the most acclaim you will ever get for it will be from the company you have over for supper who really like your homemade bread.) Yet it is probably the most optimum environment to prepare you for future life and relationships. It is probably also one of the most misunderstood places of ministry, as those around you assume that either you are being a bum who is living off your parents, or that you are wasting your talents by not going out to do whatever they think you should do.

I have experienced these responses from people—the "unglamorousness," the misunderstanding, the "be freeeeeee!!!! Do what *I* think you should do!!!" But none of these things come close to convincing me otherwise. I have seen the value of where God has placed me. I have felt the fulfillment of doing what He has given me to do. I have the security of strong relationships with those who mean the absolute most to me. I'm in the place God wants me to be. I have the freedom to go when He says go, and to stay when He says stay. I know that God is using my life experiences now to prepare me for whatever is ahead, and that as I look back on these years, they will be the complete opposite of wasted.

—MEGAN MILLER (30), keeper-at-home daughter

APPENDIX B

COLLEGE DROPOUTS HALL OF FAME

Selected and reprinted with permission from
www.collegedropoutshalloffame.com

Most young people "would be better off ... to take the four years they would have spent on college and [instead] travel, work, play, and spend time with smart people talking about important things." What is important should be your choice—not a professor or faculty committee's.

"You don't have to go to college to be a success. Even if you go for a while, you don't have to graduate to be a success. Here are just a few of the people who have become famous and/or successful without graduating from college and/or high school."

Though some of these individuals achieved worldly success rather than godly success, still their lives stand as evidence that career goals can be reached without college.

Famous, Rich, and Successful People Who Were High School or College Dropouts

Abigail Adams, U.S. first lady. Home schooled. Never went to college, though she was an avid reader.

Glenn Beck, radio and TV political commentator, bestselling book author. Enrolled at Yale University for one class but quickly dropped out because he "spent more time trying to find a parking space" than in class. He once said:

> There is such a thing as getting an education other than through the gates of a university that are charging our children $100,000 to $150,000 to $250,000 just to be able to have a certificate that doesn't necessarily mean anything to them.... I'm not anti-education. I am anti-massive debt. I am anti-giving our children's souls over to these universities.

Andrew Carnegie, industrialist and philanthropist. Elementary school dropout. Started work at the age of 13 as a bobbin boy in a textile mill. One of the first mega-billionaires in the U.S. Never went to college.

Winston Churchill, British prime minister, historian, artist. Flunked sixth grade. After he left, he applied to the Royal Military Academy at Sandhurst, but it took him three times before he passed the entrance exam. He graduated 8th out of a class of 150 a year and a half later. He never attended college.

Grover Cleveland, 22nd and 24th U.S. President. Dropped out of school to help his family. Studied law while clerking at a law firm. (Of the 43 people who served as president of the United States, 8 never went to college.)

Michael Dell, founder of Dell Computers, billionaire, among the top ten wealthiest Americans. Founded his company out of his college dorm room and dropped out of the University of Texas at the age of 19 to run the company.

Clint Eastwood, Oscar-winning actor, director, and producer. Enrolled at Los Angeles City College, but never graduated. Among other jobs, he bagged groceries, delivered papers, fought forest fires, dug swimming pools, and worked as a steelworker and a logger.

Benjamin Franklin, inventor, scientist, diplomat, author, printer, publisher, politician, patriot, signer of the U.S. Declaration of Independence. Dropped out of Boston Latin. Homeschooled with less than two years of formal education.

Robert Frost, poet. Dropped out of Dartmouth College.

Bill Gates, billionaire, co-founder of Microsoft, one of the richest men in the world, philanthropist. Even though he was only 10 points away from a perfect score on the SAT,[1] he dropped out of Harvard after his second year to work with Paul Allen on the venture that became Microsoft. As he noted, "I realized the error of my ways and decided I could make do with a high school diploma." *Time Magazine* reports:

In 2007, more than thirty years after he left Harvard, [he received] his degree (an honorary doctorate) from his alma mater. At the commencement, Gates said, "I'm a bad influence. That's why I was invited to speak at your graduation. If I had spoken at your orientation, fewer of you might be here today."[2]

George Gershwin, composer. High school dropout.

Barry Goldwater, U.S. senator and presidential candidate. He dropped out of the University of Arizona after one year to take over the family department store.

Patrick Henry, Virginia governor, revolutionary patriot. Home schooled. Later studied on his own and became a lawyer.

Andrew Jackson, U.S. president, general, attorney, judge, congressman. Orphaned at 14. Home schooled. By the age of 35, without formal education, he became a practicing attorney, military governor, Army commander, and a congressman.

Steve Jobs, billionaire co-founder of Apple Computers and Pixar Animation "dropped out of Reed College after just six months because of the undue financial strain it placed on his working-class parents' savings."[3] As he said, "I had no idea what I wanted to do with my life and how college was going to help me figure it out." So he quit college.

Andrew Johnson, 17th U.S. President, Vice-President. Never attended college.

Thomas Kincade, the painter of light, inspirational speaker, and house designer. Attended the University of California at Berkeley and the Art Center College of Design for brief periods but dropped out to become a set painter in Hollywood.

Eartha Kitt, Emmy-winning actress, dancer, singer, author. She dropped out of the High School of Performing Arts to take various odd jobs. Eventually landed a job with the Katherine Dunham dance troupe. She said, *"I am learning all the time. The tombstone will be my diploma."*

Ralph Lauren, billionaire fashion designer, founder of Polo. Left the City College of New York business school (Baruch College) to design ties for Beau Brummel. Launched Polo later that same year.

Rush Limbaugh, multi-millionaire media mogul, the most popular radio talk show host ever, bestselling book author. Dropped out of college after being required to take ballroom dancing.

Abraham Lincoln, lawyer, 16th U.S. President. Finished barely a year of formal schooling. He taught himself trigonometry (for his work as a surveyor) and read Blackstone on his own to become a lawyer.

Charles Lindbergh, aviator, first person to fly solo across the Atlantic Ocean. Quit the University of Wisconsin after two years, to learn how to fly an airplane.

Florence Nightingale, nurse. No formal education. Home schooled.

Joel Osteen, TV pastor and host of the most-watched inspirational TV show in the U.S.. Dropped out of Oral Roberts University after one year to care for his mother (who was recovering from cancer). Has sold more than 4 million copies of his book *Your Best Life Now*.

John D. Rockefeller Sr., founder of Standard Oil, philanthropist, and history's first recorded billionaire. Dropped out of high school two months before graduation. Took some courses at a local business school.

Richard Schulze, billionaire founder of Best Buy. After high school, he sold electronics for his father's distribution company and later opened a car stereo shop. Did not attend college.

Amanda Seyfried, actress. Walked out of Fordham University on her first day of classes in 2004. As she notes, "You can learn more on your own."

William Shakespeare, playwright, poet. Only a few years of formal schooling.

Adam and Matthew Toren, the founders of YoungEntrepreneur.com. On their website, Adam tells their story:

Entrepreneurs at an early age, Matthew and I had already started six (toot toot) businesses by the time we graduated high school. We were both offered college scholarships, but turned them down – it was clear to us that college was not in our future. Within a week of graduating high school, we bought a ...café... location, which we overhauled, re-branded and turned into a hot spot; and on the 12-month we sold it for a great profit.

Harry Truman, 33rd U.S. President. Never went to college.

George Washington, 1st U.S. President, plantation owner. Ended his formal education after a few years of elementary school.

Jerry Yang, billionaire co-founder of Yahoo! Dropped out of Stanford University PhD program to create Yahoo!

Mark Zuckerberg, billionaire founder of Facebook. Dropped out of Harvard to continue working on the social networking website he founded in his dorm room in 2004.

* * * * * * *

If anyone "seriously thinks that Bill Gates or Mark Zuckerberg 'halted their intellectual development' by dropping out [of college] and starting companies, we humbly suggest that he is either vastly overestimating what most people do in college, or vastly underestimating the intellectual challenges of running a startup."[4] So stated an author of an article in *Business Insider*.

So, let this list of people encourage you that in choosing to find success outside of college, you are not, by any means, alone. Others have gone before, and their example stands as a beacon calling the rest of us on to creative ways of achieving success.

ACKNOWLEDGEMENTS

A special thank you to all who shared their personal testimonials for publication in this book. Your camaraderie encourages each of us on our journeys!

Thank you to Lynne Gullo, for making her collection of news articles about college available to me. They provided the catalyst of research that I needed when I began writing this book.

Bev Williams' dedication through the editing process was irreplaceable.

For cover design, Erin Jones' creative expertise is unbeatable. Manifold thanks to her for her patience with every little change, and willingness to meet every last-minute deadline.

Deep gratitude springs from my heart for my parents, who supported me in leaving college and pursuing uncharted alternatives such as those discussed in this book.

And finally, to my precious King and Savior, Whose ways I continually find are those of success and blessing: I offer this book to You in gratitude for keeping me Yours through my year of college, and for leading me onward from strength to strength.

Recommended Resources

Books

Jim Nelson Black, *Freefall of the American University* (Nashville, Tenn.: WND Books, 2004)

Blake Boles, *Better Than College* (Loon Lake, CA: Tells Peak Press, 2012) (available as a free download at www.better-than-college.com/)

Scott & Kris Wightman, *College Without Compromise* (St. Louis: Homeschool Sampler Publishing, 2005)

Anna Sofia Botkin and Elizabeth Botkin, *So Much More* (San Antonio, Texas: Vision Forum, 2005)

Magazines, Videos

"The College Illusion," *Whistleblower*, April 2012

The College Conspiracy documentary (NIA, 2011), (available on www.youtube.com)

Websites
(Please note: The author does not necessarily endorse everything on these sites.)

UnCollege: www.UnCollege.org

EdX: www.edxonline.org

National Program on Technology Enhanced Learning: www.nptel.iitm.ac.in

MIT Open CourseWare: www.ocw.mit.edu

ENDNOTES

INTRODUCTION

1. Doug Phillips, "Discovering Life Purpose" CD (Family Renewal Audio Library).

CHAPTER 1: SPIRITUAL TSUNAMI

1. "About our shield and logo," Harvard Computer Society, www.hcs.harvard.edu/~gsascf/shield.html.
2. Linda and Sheldon Clements, "Our Founding Institutions of Academia," www.whatyouknowmightnotbeso.com/ academia.html.
3. Richard Ellsworth Day, *Flagellant on Horseback* (Lewisville, Texas: Accelerated Christian Education, Inc., 1994), p. 57-58, emphasis added.
4. Quoted in Chuck Edwards, "Why Students Walk away from Christ and What Can be Done about It," Summit Ministries, May 24, 2005, www.summit.org/resources/truth-and-consequences/.
5. The Barna Group, "Most Twentysomethings Put Christianity on the Shelf Following Spiritually Active Teen Years," September 11, 2006, www.barna.org/barna-update/article/16-teensnext-gen/147-most-twentysomethings-put-christianity-on-the-shelf-following-spiritually-active-teen-years.

6. HERI at UCLA, "Spirituality in Higher Education: A National Study of College Students' Search for Meaning and Purpose: A Summary of Initial Findings," www.spirituality.ucla.edu/docs/reports/A%20Summary%20of%20Initial%20Findings%20(Survey%20Report).pdf.

7. Brett Kunkle, "How Many Youth are Leaving the Church?", Conversant Life, February 24, 2009, www.conversantlife.com/theology/how-many-youth-are-leaving-the-church.

8. Scott McConnell, "LifeWay Research finds reasons 18- to 22-year-olds drop out of church," August 7 2007, www.lifeway.com

9. Basil Miller, John Wesley (Minneapolis, Minnesota; Bethany House Publishers, 1943), p. 20-21.

10. "70 million out of 1.3 billion, or 5.4%, vs. 1,000 out of 43,000, or 2.3%." Chinese statistic from David Aikman's, *Jesus in Beijing*, Penn State statistic from Steve Lutz, "Higher percentage of Christians in Communist China than at Penn State?", *The SENTinel*, September 2, 2008, www.stevelutz.wordpress.com.

11. Ken Ham & Greg Hall, *Already Compromised* (Green Forest: Arkansas: Master Books, 2011), p. 127.

12. Ibid., p. 128.

13. Ibid., p. 139.

14. Ibid., p. 35.

15. Ibid., p. 42.

16. Quoted in Dennis Prager, "What Kids Now Learn in College," *National Review Online*, February 28, 2012, www.nationalreview.com/articles/292108/what-kids-now-learn-college-dennis-prager?pg=1.

17. Ibid.

18. Thomas Sowell, *Inside American Education* (USA: The Free Press, 1993), p. 59, emphasis added.

19. Robert B. Brandom, *Rorty and His Critics* (United Kingdom: Blackwell Publishing, 2000), p. 21-22, emphasis added.

20. Jeff Schaeffer, "University of Babylon" speech at Summit Ministries, Session 7, October 21, 2009.

21. Dr. Anis Shorrosh, "Twenty-Year and Twenty-Step Plan for USA—Islam Targets America," *Koenig's International News*, Islam Review, www.islamreview.com/articles/20year20step.shtml.

22. *San Ramon Valley Herald* report of a speech to California Muslims in July 1998; quoted in Daniel Pipes' NY Post article, "CAIR: Moderate Friends of Terror," April 22, 2002; quoted in David Rubin, The Islamic Tsunami (USA: Shiloh Israel Press, 2010), p. 175.

23. Geert Wilders, Fitna film; quoted in David Rubin, *The Islamic Tsunami* (USA: Shiloh Israel Press, 2010), p. 227.

24. Conducted by Americans for Victory Over Terrorism, chaired by William Bennett, Jim Nelson Black, *Freefall of the American University* (Nashville, Tenn.: WND Books, 2004), p. 238.

25. David Rubin, *The Islamic Tsunami* (USA: Shiloh Israel Press, 2010), p. 123, emphasis added.

CHAPTER 2: MORAL MAELSTROM

1. Rob, "Logos in Motion," Summit Semester student blog, December 2, 2011, www.summit.org/blogs/summit-semester.

2 "Ethics, Enron, and American Higher Education: An Nas/Zogby Poll of College Seniors," *National Association of Scholars*, July 2, 2002, www.nas.org/articles.

3. Bradford Wilson, "Free Speech, Civility, and the Campus Community," National Association of Scholars, September 9, 2003; quoted in Jim Nelson Black, *Freefall of the American University* (Nashville, Tenn.: WND Books, 2004), p. 249.

4. David Kupelian, editorial, "The College Illusion," p. 4, *Whistleblower*, April 2012, Vol. 21, No. 4.

5. Jim Nelson Black, *Freefall of the American University* (Nashville, Tenn.: WND Books, 2004), p. 196.

6. Jesse Monteagudo, "The Crimson Letter: Harvard, Homosexuality and the Shaping of American Culture," International Gay & Lesbian Review (Los Angeles, CA), originally published in Gay Today (Vol. VII Issue 162).

7. Randy Thomasson, quoted in Bob Unruh, "Colleges as 'Boot Camps' For Gay Activists: 'Queer Studies' Amount to LGBT Indoctrination Program," "The College Illusion," p. 16-17, *Whistleblower*, April 2012, Vol. 21, No. 4.

8. Ibid.

9. "Dear Wheaton Students," www.onewheaton.com/letter.html.

10. Dave Bohon, "Christian Colleges are Latest Target of Homosexual Activists," *The New American*, May 9, 2011, www.thenewamerican.com/culture/education.

11. Elizabeth Dias, "Wheaton's (Unofficial) Homecoming for Gay Evangelicals", *Time U.S.*, October 7, 2011, www.time.com/time/nation.

12. Cathleen Falsani, "On evangelical campuses, rumblings of gay acceptance," *The Christian Century*, March 01, 2011, www.christiancentury.org.

13. Cathleen Falsani, "On Evangelical Campuses, Rumblings of Gay Acceptance," *The Christian Century*, March 01, 2011, www.christiancentury.org.

14. Westmont Community Life Statement www.westmont.edu /_offices/human_resources/community-life-statement.html, emphasis added.

15. Max Brantley, "God and Gays at Harding University," *Arkansas Times*, March 2, 2011, www.arktimes.com/ArkansasBlog/archives.

16. Erik Eckholm, "Even on Religious Campuses, Students Fight for Gay Identity," *The New York Times*, April 18, 2011, emphasis added.

17. Robert H. Bork, *Slouching Towards Gomorrah* (New York: Regan Books, Harper Collins Publishers, 1996), p. 3.

18. Matthew Henry, commentary on Judges 19, www.blueletterbible.org.

19. Jim Nelson Black, *Freefall of the American University* (Nashville, Tenn.: WND Books, 2004), p. 59.

20. "The Decline of Marriage and Rise of New Families," Pew Research Center, November 18, 2010, www.pewsocialtrends.org.

21. Child Trends Analysis of National Vital Statistics Data; quoted in Jason DeParle and Sabrina Tavernise, "For Women Under 30, Most Births Occur Outside Marriage," *The New York Times*, February 17, 2012.

22. Jennifer Roback Morse, Breakpoint This Week, March 11, 2012, www.breakpoint.org/features-columns/discourse/entry/15/18940.

23. Randy Alcorn, *The Purity Principle* (Sisters, Oregon: Multnomah Publishers, 2003), p. 16.

24. Joshua Harris, *Not Even a Hint* (Sisters, Oregon: Multnomah Publishers, 2003), p. 27.

25. Susan Donaldson James, "Adderall Abuse Alters Brain, Claims a Young Life," *ABC News*, November 8, 2010, www.abcnews.go.com.

26. Department of Health and Human Services, "College Health and Safety," Centers for Disease Control and Prevention, www.cdc.gov/family/college.

27. Little Richard, *Dallas Times Herald*, October 29, 1978, 14A.

28. Amy Carmichael, *God's Missionary* (CLC Publications, 2010; Reprint of Dohnavur Fellowship, 1939), p. 29.

CHAPTER 3: ACADEMIC ASSAULT

1. Joseph Farah, "The Very High Cost of Education," "The College Illusion," p. 6, *Whistleblower*, April 2012, Vol. 21, No. 4.

2. Speech at Summit Ministries, Session 7, August 21, 2009.

3. Quoted in Jim Nelson Black, *Freefall of the American University* (Nashville, Tenn.: WND Books, 2004), p. 258.

4. David Horowitz and Eli Lehrer, "Major Study Proves the Left Owns America's Colleges," "The College Illusion," p. 19-20, *Whistleblower*, April 2012, Vol. 21, No. 4.

5. Ibid.

6. David Kupelian, editorial, "The College Illusion," p. 4, *Whistleblower*, April 2012, Vol. 21, No. 4.

7. David Horowitz and Eli Lehrer, "Major Study Proves the Left Owns America's Colleges," "The College Illusion," p. 19-20, *Whistleblower*, April 2012, Vol. 21, No. 4.

8. Ibid.

9. Stephen Garber, *Fabric of Faithfulness: Weaving Together Belief & Behavior During the University Years* (Downers Grove, Illinois: InterVarsity Press, 1997), p. 77.

10. Ibid., p. 68.

11. Phyllis Schlafly, "Is College Really Worth It?", "The College Illusion," p. 31, *Whistleblower*, April 2012, Vol. 21, No. 4.

12. Robert J. Samuelson, "It's time to drop the college-for-all crusade," *The Washington Post*, May 27, 2012, www.washingtonpost.com/opinions.

13. Ibid., p. 4.

14. Janie Cheaney, "Boastful Dunces," *World Magazine*, March 28, 2009, Vol. 24, No. 6.

15. Edward Gibbon, quoted in Basil Miller, *John Wesley* (Minneapolis, Minnesota: Bethany House Publishers, 1943), p. 20.

16. Stuart Rojstaczer & Christopher Healy, "Where A Is Ordinary: The Evolution of American College and University Grading, 1940–2009," *Teachers College Record*, Vol. 114, No. 7, 2012, www.tcrecord.org/content.asp?contentid=16473.

17. Quoted in Jim Nelson Black, *Freefall of the American University* (Nashville, Tenn.: WND Books, 2004), p. 45.

18. Paul Vitz, et al, "A Nation at Risk," A Report of the National Commission on Excellence in Education. Washington, DC: U.S. Department of Education, 1983, quoted in: Ibid., p. 9.

19. Thomas Sowell, "The Dangers of 'Higher Education,'" "The College Illusion," p. 12-13, *Whistleblower*, April 2012, Vol. 21, No. 4.

20. Jim Nelson Black, *Freefall of the American University* (Nashville, Tenn.: WND Books, 2004), p. 40.

21. Jim Nelson Black, *Freefall of the American University* (Nashville, Tenn.: WND Books, 2004), p. xiv.

22. Joyce Milton, *The Road to Malpsychia* (San Fransisco: Encounter Books, 2002), p. 257.

23. Jim Nelson Black, *Freefall of the American University* (Nashville, Tenn.: WND Books, 2004), p. 136.

24. Ibid., p. 124, 152-8.

25. Dennis Prager, "What Kids Now Learn in College," February 28, 2012, www.nationalreview.com/articles/ 292108/what-kids-now-learn-college-dennis-prager?pg=1

26. Ibid.

27. Jim Nelson Black, *Freefall of the American University* (Nashville, Tenn.: WND Books, 2004), p. 33.

28. Ben Shapiro, "Sex in the Classroom: 'Homosexuality is perfectly normal. Pedophilia is acceptable. Bestiality is fine,' " "The College Illusion," p. 22, *Whistleblower*, April 2012, Vol. 21, No. 4.

29. Jeff Pollard, *Christian Modesty and the Public Undressing of America* (San Antonio, Texas: The Vision Forum, Inc.) p. 34.

30. David Kupelian, *The Marketing of Evil* (Nashville: WND Books, 2005), p. 209.

31. Antonio Weiss, "Harold Bloom: The Art of Criticism I," p. 178-232, *Paris Review*, Spring 1991, Vol. 33, No. 118, www.prelectur.stanford.edu/lecturers/bloom/ interviews.html.

32. Appendix C, Terry Mortenson and Bodie Hodge, "The Documentary Hypothesis," in Ken Ham & Greg Hall, *Already Compromised* (Green Forest, Arkansas: Master Books, 2011), p. 215.

33. Ibid., p. 225.

34. Geoffrey T. Bull, *God Holds the Key* (Chicago: Moody Press, 1959), p. 143.

35. Kenneth R. Miller, *Finding Darwin's God: A Scientist's Search for Common Ground Between God and Evolution* (New York: Harper Perennial, 1999), p. 19, 184.

36. Geoffrey T. Bull, *God Holds the Key* (Chicago: Moody Press, 1959), p. 137.

37. Jane Addams, "The Snare of Preparation," in *Twenty Years at Hull-House with Autobiographical Notes*. (New York: The MacMillan Company, 1912, c.1910), p. 65-88. www.digital.library.upenn.edu/women/addams/hullhouse/hullhouse-04.html.

38. William Deresiewicz, "The Disadvantages of an Elite Education," *The American Scholar*, Summer 2008, www.theamericanscholar.org/the-disadvantages-of-an-elite-education/

CHAPTER 4: FINANCIAL FREEFALL

1. Jennifer Ludden, "School Debt A Long-Term Burden For Many Graduates," *NPR*, October 21, 2011, www.npr.org.

2. Federal data from Fox Business analyst Gerri Willis. Whistleblower editors, "Obama Overselling College," "The College Illusion," p. 39, *Whistleblower*, April 2012, Vol. 21, No. 4, emphasis added.

3. "35 Shocking Facts That Prove That College Education Has Become A Giant Money Making Scam," The American Dream, www.endoftheamericandream.com/ archives/35-shocking-facts-that-prove-that-college-education-has-become-a-giant-money-making-scam, emphasis added.

4. Accounting Principals Workonomix Survey Series: *Post-Graduation Debt & Spending*, June 19, 2012, www.accountingprinciples.com.

5. Findings by the Federal Reserve Bank of New York Consumer Credit Panel based on overall student loan debt as of third-quarter 2011. Published by the New York Fed's Liberty Street Economics blog. Quoted in: Whistleblower editors, "Student Loans Now Surpass Credit Card Debt," "The College Illusion," p. 31, *Whistleblower*, April 2012, Vol. 21, No. 4.

6. Gary Varvel cartoon, www.cartoonistgroup.com/store/add.php?iid=64843#second, August 25, 2011.

7. Marvin Olasky, "College Bubble," World Magazine, January 14, 2012, Vol. 27, No. 1.

8. Jim Nelson Black, *Freefall of the American University* (Nashville, Tenn.: WND Books, 2004), p. 15.

9. Association of American Medical Colleges, "Tuition and Student Fees Reports," www.services.aamc.org/tsfreports/report.cfm?select_control=PRI&year_of_study=2012.

10. Robert J. Samuelson, "It's time to drop the college-for-all crusade," *The Washington Post*, www.washingtonpost.com/opinions/.

11. Mark Schneider, vice president of the American Institutes for Research, quoted in Kathy Kristof, "The Great College Hoax," *Forbes Magazine*, February 02, 2009.

12. Marvin Olasky, "College Bubble," *World Magazine*, January 14, 2012, Vol. 27, No. 1.

13. Ibid.

14. CareerBuilder.com, "20 great jobs that don't require a degree," *CNN*, February 24, 2006, www.cnn.com.

15. Jed Graham, "New Normal: Majority Of Unemployed Attended College," *Investor's Business Daily*, May 17, 2012.

16. Terence P. Jeffrey, "Out of College, Out of Work: Number of College Grads With Jobs Dropped 406,000 in June," July 6, 2012, www.cnsnews.com.

17. Kathy Kristof, "The Great College Hoax," *Forbes Magazine*, February 02, 2009.

18. People on welfare with master's degrees climbed from 101,682 to 293,029, and the number of people on welfare with Ph.D.'s went from 9,776 to 33,655, according to research from Austin Nichols, with the Urban Institute. Based on the 2008 and 2011 Current Population Surveys done by the U.S. Census Bureau and the U.S. Bureau of Labor (https://chronicle.com/article/From-Graduate-School-to/131795/).

19. Robin Wilson, "Masters in English, Will Mow Lawns," *Chronicle of Higher Education* November 28, 2010, www.chronicle.com.

20. Dixie Sommers and James C. Franklin, "Employment outlook: 2010–2020, Overview of projections to 2020,"

Monthly Labor Review, January 2012, www.bls.gov/opub/mlr/2012/01/art1full.pdf.

21. Quoted in Karin Kasdin, "Alternatives To College: Succeeding Without Higher Education," The Huffington Post, January 24, 2012.

22. Phyllis Schlafly, "College: A Dangerous Place for Men," "The College Illusion," p. 41, *Whistleblower*, April 2012, Vol. 21, No. 4.

23. Jordan Lorence, Alliance Defense Fund Senior Vice President; Senior Counsel - University Project, "Do You Want to Go Into Debt for This?", http://blog.speakupmovement.org/university/, March 2nd, 2012.

CHAPTER 5: MISPLACED MISSIONARIES

1. Bob Unruh, "Lose Christianity or Face Expulsion," *World Net Daily*, July 22, 2010, www.wnd.com/2010/ 07/182441/, emphasis added.

2. Ibid.

3. Helen Andelin, *Fascinating Womanhood* (USA/Canada: Bantam Books, 1992), p. 286.

CHAPTER 6: CHUCKING COLLEGE

1. Charles Murray, "For Most People, College is a Waste of Time," *Wall Street Journal*, August 13, 2008.

2. Kathleen Tracy, "Showcasing the Arts," *Net Places*, www.netplaces.com/jacqueline-kennedy-onassis/a-new-kind-of-white-house/showcasing-the-arts.htm, accessed May 16, 2012.

3. Art Moore, "Higher Education the Next Bubble to Burst?", "The College Illusion," p. 11, *Whistleblower*, April 2012, Vol. 21, No. 4.

4. S.M. Davis, "Victory over the Dating Spirit" CD.

5. Geoffrey T. Bull, *God Holds the Key* (Chicago: Moody Press, 1959), p. 163.

6. The Voice of the Martyrs, *Extreme Devotion* (Knoxville, Tenn.: W Publishing Group, 2001), p. 7.

7. Geoffrey T. Bull, *God Holds the Key* (Chicago: Moody Press, 1959), p. 123.

8. Ibid., p. 34.

9. Sarah Jackson, *Letters to a Young Christian* (Dahlonega, Georgia: Crown Rights Book Company, 2006; Reprint of New York: American Female Guardian Society, 1852), p. 94.

10. Geoffrey T. Bull, *God Holds the Key* (Chicago: Moody Press, 1959), p. 162.

11. Mike Clayton, "Yeshua, Son of Man, Son of God" CD.

12. Keith Green, "Why YOU Should Go to The Mission Field," 1982.

13. Hebrews 11:38.

14. David Kupelian, editorial, "The College Illusion," *Whistleblower*, April 2012, Vol. 21, No. 4.

15. Frances R. Havergal, *Kept for the Master's Use* (Bessemer, Mich.: Keepers of the Faith, reprint from 1879), p. 20.

CHAPTER 7: VOCATIONAL VISION

1. Helen Andelin, Fascinating Womanhood (USA/Canada: Bantam Books, 1992), p. 282.

2. Ibid., p. 283.

3. Ibid., p. 284.

4. Ibid., p. 286.

5. Ibid., p. 296.

6. Ibid., p.295.

7. Ibid., p. 290.

8. Jasmine Baucham, *Joyfully at Home* (San Antonio, Texas: Vision Forum, Inc., 2010), p. 145-146.

9. Patrice Lewis, "A College Degree? Not for My Kid," "The College Illusion," p. 45, *Whistleblower*, April 2012, Vol. 21, No. 4.

10. "Why You Don't Need a College Degree," www.learnfinancialplanning.com/why-you-dont-need-a-college-degree.

1. Jordan Weissmann, "The Single Most Important Experiment in Higher Education," *The Atlantic*, July 18, 2012, www.theatlantic.com/business.

CHAPTER 8: AN EXCEPTIONAL EDUCATION

2. Christopher Lasch, *The Culture of Narcissism: American Life in an Age of Diminishing Expectations* (New York: Warner Books, 1980); quoted in Jim Nelson Black, *Freefall of the American University* (Nashville, Tenn.: WND Books, 2004), p.

3. David Cohen, "Why Blake Had To Break the Rules of College to Achieve His Life Goals," www.collegeplus.org/blog.

4. Tiffany M. Schlichter, *Noble Girlhood: Becoming a Daughter of Victory & Virtue* (Virtuous Daughters, 2006), p. 203.

5. Isaac Watts, quoted in: Charles Ludwig, *Michael Faraday: Father of Electronics* (Scottdale, Penn./Waterloo, Ontario: Herald Press, 1978), p. 87.

6. Harvey Newcomb, *A Practical Directory: Helpful Instructions for Young Christian Females* (Dahlonega, Georgia: Crown Rights Book Company, 2006; Reprint of Boston: Massachusetts Sabbath School Society, 1851), p. 141.

7. Ibid., p. 142.

8. Ibid., p. 143.

9. Ibid., p. 141.

10. www.udacity.com.

11. US Department of Education, "Evaluation of Evidence-Based Practices in Online Learning," www2.ed.gov/rschstat/eval/tech/evidence-based-practices/finalreport.pdf, p. 18.

12. Marvin Olasky, "Class Without Rooms," *World Magazine*, October 10, 2009, Vol. 24, No. 20.

13. American Counsel on the Teaching of Foreign Languages, "Studies supporting increased academic achievement," www.actfl.org/i4a/pages/Index.cfm?pageID=4525#satact.

14. "Bilingualism Delays Onset of Alzheimer's Symptoms, Study Finds," ScienceDaily, November 8, 2010, www.sciencedaily.com/releases/2010/11/101108161226.htm.

15. Daniel B. Smith, "The University Has No Clothes," *New York Magazine*, May 1, 2011, www.nymag.com/news/features/college-education-2011-5/index2.html.

CHAPTER 9: EXCELLING IN ENTREPRENEURSHIP

1. "Dropping out: Is college worth the cost?", CBS News 60 Minutes, May 20, 2012, www.cbsnews.com/8301-18560_162-57436775/dropping-out-is-college-worth-the-cost/?pageNum=2&tag=contentMain;contentBody.

2. Ibid.

3. www.thielfellowship.org.

4. Ibid.

5. Ibid.

6. Anya Kamenetz, "Peter Thiel Gives Whiz Kids $100K To Quit College, Start Businesses," May 25, 2011, www.fastcompany.com/1755089/legendary-investor-peter-thiel-names-dream-team-of-whiz-kids.

7. Ibid.

8. Phil Lancaster, "The Tenets of biblical Patriarchy," Vision Forum, www.visionforumministries.org/home/about/biblical_patriarchy.aspx.

9. Matthew Henry, commentary on Proverbs 31, www.blueletterbible.org.

10. Albert C. Outler, ed., "The Use of Money," in *John Wesley*, (New York: Oxford University Press, 1964), p. 245.

11. Ibid., p. 242.

12. Albert C. Outler, ed., "The Use of Money," in *John Wesley*, (New York: Oxford University Press, 1964), p. 245.

13. Ibid.

14. John Kremer, www.collegedropoutshalloffame.com.

CHAPTER 10: THE M.R.S. DEGREE

1. Glenn T. Stanton, *The Ring Makes All the Difference* (Chicago: Moody Publishers, 2011), p. 102.

2. Germaine Greer, *The Female Eunuch* (New York: McGraw-Hill, 1971), p. 358.

3. Ibid., p. 361.

4. Linda Gordon, "Functions of the Family," *WOMEN: A Journal of Liberation,* Fall 1969.

5. Charles Krauthammer, Washington Post Writers Group, "The Aftereffects Of Feminism: Equality And Childlessness," *Chicago Tribune*, May 15, 2000.

6. Glenn T. Stanton, *The Ring Makes all the Difference* (Chicago: Moody Press, 2011), p. 143.

7. Louisa May Alcott, *Little Women* (New York: Grosset & Dunlap, 1947), Chapter 42, p. 484-5.

CHAPTER 11: SURVEYING SUCCESS

1. Randy Alcorn, *The Treasure Principle* (Sisters, Oregon: Multnomah Publishers, 2001), p. 115.

APPENDIX B: COLLEGE DROPOUTS HALL OF FAME

1. "10 Famous People Who Didn't Go to College," Financial Planning, www.learnfinancialplanning.com/famous-people-who-didnt-go-to-college/.

2. Joseph Lin, "Top 10 College Dropouts," Time, May 10, 2010, www.time.com.

3. Ibid.

4. Nick Saint, "Yes, It's Okay To Drop Out Of College," *Business Insider*, October 18, 2010, www.articles.businessinsider.com/2010-10-18/tech/29998621_1_young-people-knowledge-dropouts.

Made in the USA
Lexington, KY
29 October 2013